# Why the Rest Hates the West

MEIC PEARSE

First published in Great Britain in 2003 by
Society for Promoting Christian Knowledge
Holy Trinity Church
Marylebone Road
London NW1 4DU

British Library Cataloguing-in-Publication Data
A catalogue record for this book is available from the British Library

ISBN 0-281-05601-3

10  9  8  7  6  5  4  3  2  1

Designed and typeset by Kenneth Burnley, Wirral, Cheshire
Printed in Great Britain by Bookmarque Ltd, Croydon, Surrey

# Contents

# Preface

When the core of this book was given as a series of public lectures, it received a lively reaction. Most of it was very enthusiastic – which was disappointing, as I'd set out to make trouble. Some aspects of the encouragement were, however, truly . . . encouraging. During a coffee break, for example, a Hungarian, a Nigerian and an Indian all separately volunteered that they recognized clearly the political and social attitudes of their own countries in my description of pre-modern and non-Western societies. Most outrage was expressed by a Briton who espoused the Western ideology of human rights and insisted that, among non-Westerners, only 'extremists' thought otherwise. This was the kind of blinkered, imperialist mind-set I had intended to question and annoy. How far I have succeeded in the expanded edition of the lectures that this present book enshrines must be left to the reader's blood pressure to judge.

I have been helped in the long, slow process of writing this book by friends who have talked with me over many of the issues that it raises. Some of those discussions have been played out over years, and others only recently. Peter Heslam offered healthy encouragement, pushed some useful material in my direction, and asked one or two really hard questions. Though I have probably failed to give adequate answers to the latter – thank you! Anna Robbins helpfully punched a hole in my trial run at 'Killing the past', saving me from at least one piece of embarrassment at the stage of publication. Peter Riddell challenged me to explain myself more clearly about 'Western self-loathing' – though I doubt whether what I say would satisfy him even now. But you tried, Peter! Some of the folk at Houghton College, New York were a real blessing and encouragement, among whom Cate O'Brien, Jon Beardsley and Cameron Airhart have to get a special mention. Luiza Chandy's enthusiasm helped me to think through the implications of Wendy Shalit's amazing book. Others contributed as much or more – though only they (and perhaps not even they) know quite how much. If I live to be 90, I shall still be telling them the same thing.

# Introduction

Tolerance is a fine thing – if you can get it. That, apparently, is what distinguishes us in the West from our various recent and present antagonists around the globe, whether Saddam's Iraq, the Afghan Taliban or Kim Jong-Il's North Korea. The war against terrorism is a war against the enemies of freedom. Tolerance and openness are, so British and US political leaders like to remind their electorates, the key distinctives of the Western way of life. They are at the core of what, in recent years, such leaders have often referred to as 'our values'.

I'm not so sure. Is tolerance a 'distinctive'? It might more reasonably be called an 'in-distinctive'. It is an agreement that a previously monolithic society makes with a minority: we will tolerate you and your strange ways for reasons that seem good to us (because we think it just, or because the advantages of doing so outweigh the disadvantages – or whatever) at the price of our overall culture being a little less sharply and rigidly defined than it has been hitherto. Now, we agree to smudge the edges so that we can include you.

Or maybe, instead of this scenario, there never was a monolith in the first place. Perhaps a lot of minorities come together – as with the example of the USA – and agree to tolerate one another's funny ideas and habits. But in the process they become, for outsiders, hard to describe as a collectivity. Their culture becomes indistinct. And internally, the different minorities' sub-cultures are subjected, over time, to the 'melting-pot' effect. The USA could manage even this, partly because of its sheer size, which allowed the separate sub-cultures to maintain their existence, albeit in greatly modified form, and partly because, in their wisdom, the founding fathers greatly restricted the powers of government to interfere in the lives of its citizens.

The fact remains, however, that tolerance is a feature that, unless it is unique to one country, makes a country indistinct from others – especially over time. This, of course, may be a price well worth paying if the alternative is intolerance. And if the matter were to be left there, this would all be fine; the down-side would be more than outweighed by the up-side. Indeed, the diversity would be positively enriching, as most pluralist societies have found, to their great gain.

Unfortunately, however, this is not the end of the story. The currency of the term 'tolerance' has recently become badly debased. Where it used to mean the respecting of real, hard difference, it has come to mean instead a dogmatic abdication of claims of truth and a moralistic adherence to moral relativism, departure from either of which is stigmatized as 'intolerance'.

Whatever the causes or the justice of this shift, the fact of it is indisputable. With it, the underpinnings of the various sub-cultures are knocked away. Where the old tolerance allowed hard differences on religion and morality to rub shoulders and compete freely in the public square, the new variety wishes to lock them all indoors as matters of private judgement; the public square must be given over to indistinctness. If the old tolerance was, at least, a real value, the new, intolerant 'tolerance' might better be described as an anti-value; it is a disposition of hostility to any suggestion that one thing is 'better' than another, or even that any way of life needs protected space from its alternatives.

With this shift, the threat to distinctness becomes greatly

exacerbated. It is not just totalitarian ideologues who will come into conflict with us Westerners; anyone who cares about their culture, and who has enough exposure to us and our way of doing things to be affected by us, will feel threatened.

The same can be said of 'openness'. The American academic Allan Bloom, after a lifetime of teaching under-graduate students, found the relapse into bland, content-less 'niceness' to be the death of any meaningful intellectual life. He described it this way:

> Openness – and the relativism that makes it the only
> plausible stance in the face of various claims to truth and
> various ways of life and kinds of human beings –
> is the great insight of our times. The true believer is the
> real danger. The study of history and of culture teaches
> that all the world was mad in the past; men always
> thought they were right, and that led to wars, persecu-
> tions, slavery, xenophobia, racism and chauvinism.
> The point is not to correct the mistakes and really be
> right; rather it is not to think you are right at all.[1]

His book *The Closing of the American Mind* was an all-out assault upon this dogmatic nescience. For 'openness', by def-inition, excludes the possibility of closing on the truth – because then you are no longer open. It is therefore hostile to 'hard' truth claims. Although this fixed 'openness' is very compatible with the new meaning of 'tolerance', it renders the original meaning absurd.

Openness, then, is not a value, but an anti-value. Our politicians' claims notwithstanding, it cannot be part of 'our identity', because it excludes all hard definitions of identity, and by its insistent hyper-inclusivity, it destroys any real meaning of 'we' (because it cannot be distinguished from 'non-we'). Hence its accompanying prattle about 'commu-nity' is rendered meaningless. And if we cannot see that point, non-Westerners certainly can.

Despite these problems, in the past 20 years or so 'tolerance' (new-style) and 'openness' have passed beyond the stage of being consciously held ideals in Western countries; they have become foundational to the Western outlook. The person who does not hold them is increasingly looked upon with bafflement or disbelief. They have become part of 'common sense'.

And what, pray, is that? 'Common sense', like a presupposition, is what we think before we think we're thinking. (You may want to read that sentence again!) It is the common stock of presuppositions current in one's own particular society. Some of those ideas are doubtless genuinely 'common' in the sense that all human communities really have shared them. Dropped objects fall to the ground. Death and pain are everywhere ordinarily to be avoided. Any culture that ignored these truisms would not endure, and so the normal state of affairs that did receive them as 'common sense' would reassert itself. (Exceptions to the avoidance of death and pain – in respect of duty, love, religious purposes and so on – are accorded appropriate solemnity or honour precisely because the occasions that trigger them are so extreme that even 'common sense' is to be laid aside.)

Some of our other presuppositions (such as, say, 'the importance of privacy'), however, are not genuinely common at all, though existentially they may appear to be so. If all of the people around us share a certain idea, sentiment, or expectation about life and social discourse, as somehow 'obvious', and if we ourselves have been brought up to share the same expectations, we shall consider it to be a part of 'common sense'. Even so, the perception in question may be one that has been current only in our own society. It may, indeed, have been current even there only for a limited amount of time. (As Patricia Crone puts it, 'We all take the world in which we were born for granted and think of the human condition as ours. This is a mistake. The vast mass of human experience has been made under quite different conditions.'[2]) However, if enough of our social world has been built around that limited bit of experience that is our own, and if it takes its truth as axiomatic, we shall be hard to persuade that it is anything other than a self-evident truth. If confronted by individuals or groups who differ from this perception and who behave accordingly, we shall probably consider them to be stupid, crazy or perhaps fanatical.

Unfortunately, this is precisely the bind in which the Western world finds itself at the start of the third millennium. Its ideas of 'common sense' – the common values shared (to differing degrees, certainly) by Western societies generally – are sharply at odds with those of the non-Western cultures that confront them. Indeed, they are sharply at odds with the values and ideas of the West's own history. To some extent, of course, this is hardly surprising. Indeed, it is what one would expect. What anybody means by a 'culture' (in the widest sense of that word) is a set of distinctive attitudes, beliefs and behaviours that distinguish it from all others. However, there are several factors that make it increasingly urgent for Westerners to obtain a clear view of what makes their own culture tick so that, seeing themselves, they can more clearly understand why the rest of the world considers them – as it most assuredly does – to be dangerously seductive but domineering barbarians.

### The oddness of Western 'common sense'

In the first place, the assumptions of the Western world-view are more sharply distinguished from those of other people than has been the case in any other major culture in history. The grounds for misunderstanding (including self-misunderstanding) and enmity towards others are greater. Put simply, a fourth-century Japanese, a fourteenth-century English peasant, an eighteenth-century Maori, a nineteenth-century Congolese and an early twentieth-century Azeri would all have had more in common with one another, both in the condition of their material lives and in their assumptions about the world and social discourse within it, than any of them would have had with early third-millennium Americans, Britons or Germans. 'Most people, and certainly most members of Western civilization, are thus born into a world which differs radically from that of their ancestors, with the result that most of human history is a closed book to them.'[3] More to our point, most contemporary non-Western experience, assumptions and values are an incomprehensible 'closed book' to Westerners also. For, to the extent that they remain un-westernized, we could have added a goodly number of contemporary Third World citizens to our list of historical exotics without altering the equation. However, most non-Westerners are, in practice, in the process of being westernized, or at least they are feeling the pressures of Western ways on their own traditional cultures. Not only does that affect the equation we have been making here, but it brings us to our next point in respect of the urgency for Westerners to understand their own underlying ideas of what constitutes 'common sense'.

For, in the second place, Westerners have been enjoying a period of global dominance during the past couple of centuries. Although that dominance is now in marked decline, the process of globalization itself – in communications, in the spread of technological developments, in economic trends, to say nothing of the movement of people – is continuing. Mutual incomprehension is a dangerous state of affairs for millions of people whose lives are increasingly bound up with one another.

For most of the nineteenth and twentieth centuries, Westerners hardly felt the need to take alternative world-views seriously, since Western values, customs and ideas seemed so obviously set to dominate the world. The outlooks of Muslims, Chinese or Hindus seemed at that time to be so much historical debris, of interest to anthropologists and museums, perhaps, but not as material for serious mental engagement or demanding to be understood in their own terms by anyone other than academic specialists or missionaries. They were but variant forms of the primitivism that, like snow in springtime, was melting away in the sunshine of Western modernity and newness. However, continuing Western economic power is now spawning not only emulation by non-Western societies, but also cultural retrenchment and confrontation. The rising tide of Islamism, both in the Islamic world and among Muslim minorities in non-Muslim countries, is merely the most prominent example of this trend. If sub-Saharan Africa seems to show a continued willingness to absorb Western influences (however ineffectually in terms of its own development), the great civilizations of Asia – Chinese, Hindu, Japanese and others – are declining the offer of further assimilation along Western lines. The collapse of Communism has led to the reassertion of Orthodox culture across wide swathes of eastern Europe. Any further globalization – of the economy or anything else – will not take place simply on the basis of an uncritical adoption of Western attitudes and values. Westerners can no longer act on the bland assumption that their ideas about what constitutes 'common sense' are universal or beyond examination.

In any case (and this brings us to our third point), the picture of Western domination is changing. The globalization continues, but the idea that this is equivalent to Westernization can no longer be taken for granted. Some statistics illustrate the point. In 1928, the West produced 84.2 per cent of all manufactured goods in the world; by 1980, this was down to 57.8 per cent. In 1950, Western countries had 64.1 per cent of total world gross economic product; by 1992, it was only 48.9 per cent. In 1920, almost one-half of the world's population – 48.1 per cent – was under the political control (including empires) of

Western governments. Now the empires are gone and populations are declining in the Western countries themselves; the comparable statistic at the start of the new millennium is around one-eighth, at 12.5 per cent. Historically, population booms are accompanied by a rise in the political influence of the country or culture that is booming, and the population boom right now (forecast to continue until the 2020s) is in the Islamic world.[4] As an illustration of the Islamic population shift and its effects, it is worth noticing that the large rise in the population of Kosovar Albanians (who are mostly Muslim) was no small factor in the long-to-medium-term causes of the Kosovo crisis, especially when one considers that the Serb birth rate was – and is – low and stagnant. According to some estimates, if Kosovo had remained fully incorporated in the Yugoslav state, Muslim Kosovar recruits would have constituted a majority in the Yugoslav army as a whole sometime in the 2030s!

## The unavoidability of cultural engagement

The significance of these shifts ought not to be underestimated. One of the most insightful, as well as one of the best-selling, books of political analysis of the 1990s was Samuel P. Huntington's masterpiece *The Clash of Civilizations and the Remaking of World Order*, which argued persuasively that the end of the Cold War and the 'death of ideology' was ushering in a return to civilizational politics. As he sees it, international co-operation and international conflict are increasingly dominated by long-term cultural factors, with alliances between cultural brethren and flashpoints along civilizational fault lines. The example of the Balkans, where three major cultures meet, is so obvious as hardly to need mentioning, but the choosing of diplomatic 'sides' by outside powers during the 1999 Kosovo crisis also fits Huntington's analysis exactly.

His polemical phrase 'the West and the rest' has recently been used, in precisely that form, as the title for Roger Scruton's latest book.[5] Both of these works, however, are concerned with comparative themes to a degree that I am not undertaking – and I would, in any case, be relatively ill-equipped to do so. Huntington is a veritable polymath, but his massive learning is directed almost entirely at the world since 1900, and I wish to dig back a little deeper and a little more narrowly; that is, I wish to pay close attention to key developments since the Reformation but to confine myself within the parameters of the West. Scruton's analysis is also very valuable, and yet he is, to my mind, a little too impressed with the idea of the nation-state, overgenerous in his assessment of its antiquity and far too optimistic in his judgements of the degree of continuing popular commitment to its civic life – or to any civic life. (For goodness' sake! Barely half the population in the UK even bothers to vote!)

The boundaries of the West may be larger than they were during the Cold War, but not by much: the Roman Catholic countries of central and eastern Europe (Poland, the Czech Republic, Hungary, Slovenia, Lithuania) can be incorporated into the structures of NATO, the European Union (EU) and so on with a minimum of fuss and bother, not because the authorities in Brussels and Strasbourg have a prejudice in favour of Roman Catholicism, but because these countries have economies, political institutions and social attitudes that are more closely consonant with those already prevailing in the West, and this consonance is rooted in the long-term shaping effects of Western Christendom. Both Hungary and Belgium, for example, are secularized societies now, yet the mind-sets of their populations have more in common with one another than either has with the mentality that is prevalent in, say, Macedonia. The same rule of long-term consonance would be true of Estonia and Latvia, which are unusual for this region in being Protestant; the contrast is not between Roman Catholicism and 'others', but between 'Western Christendom' and Eastern Orthodoxy. With the sole exception of Cyprus, all of the ten putative new entrants to the EU are parts of historic Western Christendom. (The only country part of that historic entity not yet invited to join is Croatia.) Cyprus, of course, has strong attachments to Greece, which already belongs to the EU.

Indeed, if Huntington is right, there will be several areas where the boundaries of 'the West' are actually contracting. During the Cold War, when the Soviet threat loomed large, Turkey was firmly on board. Now her alignment is more uncertain, and her condition as what Huntington calls a 'torn' country (torn, that is, between the westernizing, secular heirs of Kemal Atatürk and the rising power of the Islamists) is becoming more apparent. In view of her record in respect of human rights and a whole host of other matters, only US pressure makes Turkey acceptable for consideration as a candidate for EU membership. And the extreme ambivalence towards her application can only strengthen the hand of the supporters of Islamist retrenchment inside Turkey itself. Within the existing EU, it is Greece, the only member that is not an historical part of Western Christendom, that does not fit, whether in economic matters or the alphabet, in matters as diverse as diplomatic sympathies in the Kosovo crisis or its willingness to imprison street evangelists. On the other side of the world, Japan has been distancing itself from the close alignment with the USA and the Western world, which had been its stance during the Cold War, as it comes to terms with its own status as an economic superpower and the need to live with the newly awakened dragon on its doorstep, China.

These emerging realities will increasingly demand more cultural engagement and real understanding – by Westerners and by others – than has been common hitherto. This brings us to our fourth point in respect of the urgency of a realistic self-understanding by Westerners. Cultural debate in recent decades has been characterized by what Robert Hughes has called a 'sterile confrontation between the two PCs – the politically and the patriotically correct'.[6] The 'patriotism' refers to the specifically US form of the struggle; even so, in its wider context, the polarization he describes is broadly similar in shape on both sides of the Atlantic. On the one hand are those who, typically aligned with the political Right, defend the Western cultural legacy in all its aspects. West is best because West is right. Economic progress and modernization stem from better cultural values. At a popular level, this has been the theme of commentators such as Pat Buchanan or the American religious Right. A far more finely nuanced and intellectually substantial, but still definite case of this sort has been made by David Landes's recent book *The Wealth and Poverty of Nations*, in which he attempts to seek out the historical causes of both prosperity and its absence.[7] On the other hand, and typically aligned with the political Left, are those who rubbish the Western superiority complex, tear into the 'cultural canon' of art and literature as being the product of a misogynistic, racist, homophobic élite, and denounce Western history as it has traditionally been understood, particularly in respect of Western contacts with other cultures, as a catalogue of oppression and destruction, misrecorded by 'myths' that now demand to be replaced by 'counter-myths'.

## Bogus engagement: 'multiculturalism'

Of the two camps, the former does at least have the merit of consistency. If Western ascendancy rests on the fact that its values are rooted in a superior cultural project, then the world-wide triumph of capitalism and democracy can be expected some time soon. In point of fact, however, this myopia is challenged by those countries – Malaysia, China and, in differing degrees, other Asian economies – who have embraced the one without the other. (In fairness, it should be said that attempts to embrace the other without the one – as in parts of eastern Europe – appear to be leading to the demise of the democratic experiment.)

The decline of Western populations – a topic to which we shall return – is making increasing immigration a necessity, just to keep the economic wheels turning at home. And looking abroad, the 'new world (dis)order' is looking distinctly scarier than the Cold War that it has replaced: unstable Islam; the impending rise of China to the status of global colossus; the imponderable threats posed by rogue states such as North Korea 'going nuclear'. When these instabilities are enhanced by the likely drastic effects of global climate change upon agriculture, economics and politics in the coming decades – effects brought about, ultimately, by industrial pollution – then Western triumphalism about a superior culture and superior economics seems to be well out of order.

The latter camp, that of the politically correct brigade, is riddled with inconsistencies. Its slogan may be 'multiculturalism', but its reality is to idealize traditional cultures by cutting them into its own image and, in the process, grotesquely distorting them. 'Asian values' are OK if they are kept vague on specifics and used merely as a foil for 'Western individualism' or other whipping-boys of the fashionable Left. But if examined too closely, they prove to be even more offensive to 'correct' opinion than the Western values that have just been debunked. The battle cry of 'communitarianism' is good for attacking a new supermarket development, but if applied to family ethics we soon find that we are back to homophobia, marriage and sexual chastity.

This dilemma for the Left was excellently illustrated by the 1998 Lambeth Conference, which gathered together the bishops of the world-wide Anglican Communion. The conference surprised a number of commentators by its decision to uphold traditional biblical teaching in condemning homosexual practices, whereas it had been calculated by many that the liberal, permissive wing of the Church would predominate. However, evangelicals and other traditionalists were strengthened at the conference by the augmented battalion of bishops from the growing community of the African Church. As representatives of traditional cultures, these bishops had no problem with biblical injunctions on the subject of homosexuality, and they expressed considerable bewilderment when confronted by Westerners who did. As one of them commented, 'You came over to our country 150 years ago and gave us the Bible. Now you are telling us the Bible is not true.'

The most telling moment was when, after the motion upholding traditional teaching was passed, Jack Spong, the arch-liberal Bishop of Newark, New Jersey, denounced the African bishops as 'superstitious' and 'uneducated'.[8] It must have been a moment of madness; the politically correct, anti-racist, multiculturalist Jack Spong would never have uttered such words, even in defence of a cause so dear to the heart of the anti-homophobic Jack Spong, except under the influence of some extreme emotion. Of course, if the Africans really had been superstitious and uneducated, then only the politically correct *illuminati* would have denied the fact. For them, problems should never be addressed as problems; instead they should be sublimated into the realm of politics, thereby rendering even a frank description of the issues – let alone any possibility of resolution – impossible. In this case, however, Spong was plainly wrong on matters of fact: the African bishops were, on the whole, as educated as he. And, concerning superstition, their real offence, as far as Spong was concerned, consisted in the fact that they had dared to touch one of his sacred cows. For they had failed to come to the kind of moral judgement about homosexuality that a liberal-minded, tolerant, open Westerner – as

13

exemplified by himself – would and should have come to. In other words, the trouble with the Africans was that they were not Western enough!

The same phenomenon pervades the thinking of self-styled liberals of all kinds, and makes 'multiculturalism' a hollow mockery: good enough for belittling and relativizing those Western values that are really worthwhile and solid, while absolutizing those that are trivial, egocentric and self-destructive. One example from my own experience will serve to illustrate the trend. A medium-sized employer, which prided itself (with some justification) on its multiethnicity and its multicultural diversity, faced a choice of applicants for an important position. Located in a Western country, it was not surprising that the applicants were themselves Westerners. Almost all of them, anyway. One came from a definitely non-Western background. The fairly large, impeccably democratic and participative interviewing panel listened patiently to the presentations by the several would-be employees, and had a *post mortem* discussion among themselves after each interview. High hopes had been held of the non-Western applicant, because it was wished to broaden the ethnic and cultural diversity of the management. In the event, he was deemed hopelessly unsuitable; his relevant technical expertise was above reproach and his English flawless, though his accent required some concentration to follow; the real difficulty was that his approach to problems was considered to be outrageously prescriptivist and cut-and-dried. Like Spong's African bishops, the fellow was simply not Western enough.

This is the irony and the emptiness of 'multiculturalism'. 'Tolerant', 'open' Western cosmopolitans can get along with anyone, anywhere, on one condition: that they be westernized cosmopolitans like themselves. Non-Western values – or even Western values of more than a few decades ago – are simply not welcome at the table of discourse. And that discourse had better be in English; knowledge of that tongue by non-Anglo-Saxons is taken for granted, while knowledge of other languages by Anglo-Saxons themselves is suspect as élitist. It seems that the only parts of their culture that the non-Westerners are allowed under multiculturalism is their fancy dress and their war dances. In exchange they are taken as having given their tacit support to the Western Left in its crusade for 'communitarianism' and against 'individualism' – and thus to a rearguard action against free markets and personal responsibility after the demise of socialism and the welfare state.

## Sound presuppositions, flawed presuppositions

The main claimants to the feat of having performed a strip-tease of Western world-views, then, turn out to have achieved no such thing. The mantle having fallen, we must endeavour to pick it up. I hope, however, that I am not so naive as to think that, having identified and described some social phenomenon, or having located its origins in time and place, we have thereby debunked it. Simply identifying some idea as a (hitherto unexamined) 'presupposition' does not demonstrate the falsity of that idea. Some foundational ideas must be presupposed, or we can neither think nor act at all.

There is some merit in insisting upon the alternative meaning of the word 'presupposition' – alternative, that is, to its usual sense of 'an unexamined foundational idea that, once exposed, is presumed to be false'. It can also mean one starting point among several that we consciously choose because of its greater explanatory power. 'If we presuppose *this*', we might say, 'then the phenomena of the world around us are better, or more satisfactorily, explained than if we presuppose *that*.' If we bear in mind this meaning, then we can remember that something is not necessarily debunked by virtue of having been identified as 'a presupposition'; whether it should be retained or junked remains an entirely separate question.

Accordingly, this book constitutes neither an attack on the Western world-view as a whole, nor a defence of it. As will quickly become apparent, however, we shall find cause to approve of some aspects the more, others the less. It does, however, seem to me that fashionable Western self-loathing is fundamentally misplaced. Almost always it is directed at the fact of our wealth and power, relative to the other peoples of the earth, with the constant, quasi-Marxist (and false) assumption that the wealth must somehow inevitably be stolen from the poor, as if the economic pie were of a fixed size and economics a zero-sum game. Really, a decade and a half after the fall of communism, do we still need to go on disproving this? Our vast wealth does, indeed, impose upon us equally vast responsibilities towards those who remain in poverty. It is the real strengths of the West that created that wealth and that, tentatively and in humility, need to be proffered to those who could profit from them.

The self-loathing, however, should be redirected from the mere fact of our prosperity to the disconnection, boredom, feeble-mindedness and infantilism that we have allowed our wealth to let us slip into. The unprecedented comfort of our lives allows us, if we are not careful – and we have not been careful – to lose hold of the fundamental realities that underpin all human existence. We can, after all, use our wealth to cocoon ourselves from those unpleasant realities, at least for a while. In so doing, we fail to empathize with the poor majority of the earth's inhabitants who cannot escape, setting ourselves up for conflict with them. And, by endorsing a determined, principled naivety, we set ourselves up for eventual fall, as reality 'snaps back'.

All of this is to anticipate later chapters, however. In any case, mostly, what I am trying to do is to explain. Accordingly, I offer no opinion about the rightness or wrongness of the confrontation with Iraq, or of the 'war on terror', or about the Israel–Palestine situation. Neither do I offer any prognosis about the likely future course of events in those struggles. I am hardly without opinions on these subjects, but to express them would be immediately to start an argument about symptoms; I wish to draw attention to the causes, at least on 'our' (that is, the Western) side of the equation.

## *Economics, religion – or culture?*

Concerning the 'other' side (which means, I suppose, in our present exigency, especially the Islamic world), I would venture at least this: the kind of Western political and journalistic rhetoric that attributes anti-Westernism in general and support for al-Qaida and the attacks of 11 September 2001 in particular to economics ('It's all about global poverty') or to religion is profoundly misplaced.

To assert that economics is the root cause is wrong concerning the specific facts. Most of the terrorists of 11 September were prosperous and had benefited from Western training. Osama bin Laden's extreme wealth is well known. It is, furthermore, among the new urban middle classes of the Muslim world, not the most impoverished people in the slums or the villages, that radical Islamism thrives. Western arguments based on economic determinism stem from a discredited, quasi-Marxism to which our academic and chattering classes remain addicted, a decade after the end of communism and fully 50 years after they should have learned to know better. Marxism, of course, likes to pretend that all political, religious and cultural disputes are really economic grievances in fancy dress. Matter is all that exists, and so religion and morality are simply so much play-acting, their strictures designed to justify the economic privileges of the ruling classes. The time is long past when such reductionism might be thought to have 'explained' human actions. Economics are indeed implicated in our present troubles, but only as an exacerbation of other causes. It is hardly the only cause – or even the main cause – of the present troubles. (Sub-Saharan Africa, for example, is in a far worse economic state than the Middle East, but its struggles are all internal; they are not directed against the rich West.)

There simply is no neat fit between the Western middle classes' desire for self-loathing (on account of their own wealth and power) and the real resentments of non-Westerners – even if the latter are understandably only too happy to pander to the former in order to exert leverage.

Neither is the 'war' – if that is what this is – on terrorism simply about 'religion', even though faith is a major factor in the cocktail of conflict. Back in 1996 in Jerusalem, I had a conversation with an Israeli who insisted, in all seriousness, that Palestinian discontent was caused by Islamist radicalism. Destroy 'fundamentalism', he believed, and one would have peace between Israel and the Arabs. That the very existence of the Jewish state might be intolerable to at least some Arabs, and the actual behaviour of Israel a *casus belli* even for moderate Palestinians, seemed not to have occurred to him. His myopia is mirrored, on a global scale, by Westerners everywhere. 'Religion', it is argued, is the 'cause' of the conflict. The best resolution of the problem, such an analysis implies, would be the death – or at least the utter emasculation – of religion around the world. This view fails to take religion seriously, as if agnosticism were somehow 'obviously' more rational and peaceful than piety, an idea that the unspeakably bloody twentieth century should have laid to rest. By their constant, mindlessly inaccurate resort to the 'f'-word – fundamentalism – to describe the upsurge of religious fervour in much of the non-West, Western secularists are employing a boo-word that long ago lost its original meaning and has come to signify 'more-religious-than-I-happen-to-like' – and thus to say more about the speaker than about the persons, things or phenomena described. It is one more signifier that Western self-styled 'multiculturalists' are, in fact, refusing to take seriously any culture but their own. The insistence that the conflict is all about religion also ignores the rather obvious point that the religious anger is part of a response to something wider.

It is much more strongly arguable that anti-Westernism (among Muslims, at least) is due to Western foreign policies: support for Israel; the propping up of non-Islamist regimes in the Muslim world; war and sanctions against Iraq; US forces 'contaminating' the holy soil of Arabia with their infidel presence. These things are difficult to disentangle. No one seriously expects any state to pursue anything other than self-interest in foreign policy. It is hard to see how Western governments could accommodate these grievances. It is likely that further demands would follow swiftly on their heels – though (since abandonment of support for the existence, at least, of Israel is in practice unthinkable) we are hardly likely to find out.

My contention, however, is that the primary cause of the conflict is cultural. And 'culture', of course, includes religion, but also much else besides. Non-Westerners are becoming understandably anxious about the future of their cultural space, which they feel is being intolerably threatened by aliens – that is, by us. And to the non-West our culture appears not as a culture at all but as an anti-culture. Our values appear not as an alternative to traditional values but as a negation of them – as anti-values, in fact.

The truth is that we, in our hyper-prosperity, may be able to live without meaning, faith or purpose, filling our three score years and ten with a variety of entertainments – but most of the world cannot. If economics is implicated in the conflict, it is mostly in an ironic sense: only an abundance of riches such as no previous generation has known could possibly console us for the emptiness of our lives, the absence of stable families and relationships and the lack of any over-arching purpose. And even within us, the pampered babies who populate the West, something – rather a big something – keeps rebelling against the hollowness of it all. But then our next consumer goodie comes along and keeps us happy and distracted for the next five minutes. Normal people (that is, the rest of the world), however, cannot exist without real meaning, without religion anchored in something deeper than existentialism and bland niceness, without a culture rooted deep in the soil of the place where they live. Yet it is these things that globalization is threatening to demolish. And we wonder that they are angry?

# Barbarian juggernauts

### Two truck rides

It was 1982, and the Western powers – or an assortment of them – had finally taken it upon themselves to intervene in Lebanon's long-running civil war. The US and French forces were attempting to hold the ring in the face of multi-factional anarchy and mayhem. It was in this context that a truck bomb was delivered, with devastating effect, into the heart of the US marine barracks. The bomber burst his vehicle through the gates, drove up to the building, and blew himself and more than two hundred Americans into eternity. The stunned guard at the entrance to the compound was interviewed afterwards. Too late he had realized what was happening. Too late he had grasped that the man at the wheel was a bomber who was successfully penetrating the outer cordon. As the truck driver drove past the guard, the latter reminisced, 'he was smiling'.

He might well have smiled. For him, his own death would long ago have been settled in his mind as a price worth paying for immolating a large number of Americans. He had planned this mission for some time. As he drove through the gates, he knew that he had succeeded. Too late, the guard knew it too.

But what kind of hatred drove the truck driver to this appalling act? That participants in the civil war may have wished to continue their feuding around and in spite of the outside occupiers is understandable. That minor frictions between locals and peacekeepers could occur with the latter caught in the factional crossfire is also unsurprising. But why this?

Too many Westerners take refuge in simplistic explanations: fanaticism, extremism, 'fundamentalism', insanity. Such dismissals advance the task of comprehension not one jot; they reveal more about the speaker than about the things, or the persons, described. They indicate, not so much an understanding, as a refusal to understand. All of these epithets indicate, in practice if not quite in theory, a mental banishment: 'these things are so far distant from my own feelings or judgements that I shall make no attempt to comprehend them in their own terms or to understand why these people, in their own estimation, act or think as they do.' And thus we are condemned either to complete separation from cross-cultural entanglements or else (since that is virtually impossible in the face of globalization) to the recurrence of such disasters.

Let no one misconstrue this use of the word 'understand'. No implication of condoning whatsoever is intended. There are no shades here of 'understand a little more; condemn a little less'. Only unqualified, unmitigated condemnation is appropriate in such cases. And yet there must be understanding (in the sense of mental comprehension) if we are to prevent repetition of the like horrors.

Perhaps we should pause for breath here. Those preceding paragraphs were written at the end of the 1990s – that is, before the attacks on the World Trade Center and the Pentagon on 11 September 2001. Following those terrible events, I found myself approached on two different occasions, once by a friend from church and once by two of my students, who wanted to talk the situation over with me because, they insisted, I had predicted just such attacks.

On the evening of the day itself, as the news from America began to register in London, I commented to someone that 'This is just the beginning', and was told 'Oh, don't *say* that!'

Very well. Let us not say it. Let us pretend that everything shall be well. Let us continue to ignore the real problems. Let us imagine that, if we continue to soft-soap manifestations of 'religion', non-Westerners will stand by as we absent-mindedly obliterate their cultures. After all, that is what we have been doing until now. Even after 11 September, our politicians continue to address the non-West as if all the world were Westerners under the skin; everybody wants 'freedom' and the consumerist paradise and, in order to obtain these things, considers the adoption of Western anti-values and the anti-culture to be a price well worth paying.

Let us turn our attention for a moment to a smaller, but far more hopeful and positive anecdote before turning to the general picture that unites it with the darker scenario we have been considering. This story again concerns the Arab world in the early 1980s. This one takes place in Algeria before the present troubles. A group of young Westerners from a Christian mission organization were travelling through that Muslim country, in which evangelism is strictly forbidden. These were no culturally insensitive Bible-belters, however, thinking to transplant the values of rural Missouri to the Maghreb. A multinational group acutely aware of their own ignorance and impotence in such a (to them) hostile environment, they were aiming at very modest goals indeed. Their intention was to travel through the country from north to south, from the populated coastal region, through the desert, and on into the countries of the Sahel beyond. Praying. Praying for the places they travelled through, for the people they met and for opportunities to evangelize individual people who appeared to be open to the gospel. Like the Lebanese bomber, they were travelling by truck.

The group stopped late one afternoon just beyond the last house in a village several hundred miles south of the coast. They got out, gathered round a fire, made a meal and then began singing their songs, quietly and reverently. After a couple of hours, an old man from the village came out of his house and wandered over to talk to them. He said that he had been watching them for a while, and that he was amazed. They were, he told them, unlike any Westerners he had encountered before, or had ever heard of. Why did they behave this way?

What surprised the old man? He had been expecting Westerners to make a noise, to turn their radios up, to spill Coke cans all over the desert, for their womenfolk to be baring arms and legs – or maybe more. These young people were doing none of these things. In a word, he expected them to be barbarians. It was a measure of the oddness of the occasion, and the oddness of these young people, that this time he was wrong.

## Oblivious domination

The truth is that Westerners are perceived by non-Westerners (if we can make such a huge generalization about a truly global phenomenon) as rich, technologically sophisticated, economically and politically dominant, morally contemptible barbarians. That is a hateful combination of feelings and assessments, in the sense that the one who makes them will, as often as not, be filled with hatred for the objects of such contemplation.

Why barbarians? For despising tradition, the ancestors and the dead. For despising religion, or at least for treating it lightly. For the shallowness and triviality of their culture. For their sexual shamelessness. For their loose adherence to family and, sometimes, also to tribe. For their absence of any sense of honour. These are massive charges, of course, and it is necessary, in what follows, to say something about each in turn. For the moment we simply note that they do, in point of fact, generate resentment – a resentment that can, as with the man driving the truck bomb, amount to hatred.

That is not to deny that many Western attributes and trappings are found desirable by non-Westerners. But precisely that desirability compounds the problem. Western culture, the very source of offence to traditional cultural sensibilities, has a habit of finding out the weak spots of the guardians of tradition and of undermining them from within. The allure of heightened sexuality, or of status clothing, furnishings and possessions, or of personal independence: one would have to be superhuman not to feel the pull of these things or to be tempted by them. That is why many anti-Western movements, notably Islamists, wish to banish the very presence of the Western temptations or to take a separatist line, or at least to limit contacts with Western people and institutions to what can be dictated on their own cultural terms. As one Iranian leader of Ansar-e Hezbollah put it, 'When you see some people here dressed in American-style clothes, you are seeing the bullets of the West.'[1]

Far more people than just Islamists, however, wish to modernize their countries without, at the same time, westernizing them. Samuel P. Huntington has argued at length that this is the task in which much or most of the non-West is now engaged.[2] The extreme difficulty of such an enterprise lies in the fact that the West is the historic source of modernization and its principal present agent. Modernizing without westernizing is a near-impossible task of extrication. The Internet (to take only the most obvious example) knows no boundaries. To accept the technology is to accept the presence of pornography, advertising, commercial values and freedom of speech. In response, the Taliban in

Afghanistan (admittedly one of the most extreme cases) did not shy away from banning virtually all aspects of modernity in their determination to sweep their collective house clean of Western contamination.

Very many people, especially in the Third World, have the sensation that everything they hold dear and sacred is being rolled over by an economic and cultural juggernaut that doesn't even know it's doing it . . . and wouldn't understand why what it's destroying is important or of value. That is why the defenders of traditionalism and advocates of cultural retrenchment in the non-West are perceived by Westerners as 'fanatics', 'fundamentalists' – the epithets that express a refusal to understand. Why? Because they fly in the face of what, to Westerners, is 'common sense'.

And the worst of it is, that Westerners themselves are hardly aware of what they are doing and are hardly aware of the very existence of the things that they are destroying. Many non-Westerners feel that they have some understanding of Western culture; because of television and pop music, to say nothing of the high-status artefacts on sale to those who can afford them, it would be strange indeed if they did not. Even so, the amount of understanding transmitted through these channels is likely to be superficial (life in the West being construed as somehow effortlessly prosperous); however, the level of understanding in the reverse direction – that is, the level of understanding of others by Westerners themselves – is almost negligible. After almost a decade of coverage of the Balkan wars on television, most Westerners are still unsure of the identities of the principal protagonists, and even news announcers occasionally betray the fact that they do not understand the meaning of the term 'the former Yugoslavia'. (In 2001, BBC radio introduced an interviewee as 'the Ambassador for the former Yugoslavia'. How can anyone be an ambassador for a 'former' country? Which government would one then be representing? The hapless man, knowing he faced a hopeless task, did not even bother to correct his interviewer. On another occasion in the same year, Kosovo was described as 'part of the former Yugoslavia' even though, from any conceivable legal viewpoint – including NATO's – it was still part of the *existing* Yugoslavia.) Survey after survey shows the embarrassing ignorance of even educated Americans about the most fundamental features of the world outside their own country. Supporters of tradition in the non-West have the sense that they are being rolled over by a juggernaut that does not even know they exist.

Westerners are so accustomed to this effortless superiority that the real nature of its origins are lost on them. As Huntington points out, 'The West won the world not by the superiority of its ideas or values or religion . . . but rather by its superiority in applying organized violence. Westerners often forget this fact; non-Westerners never do.'[3] Indeed, this obliviousness of reality persists, even when the present nature of international relationships is being considered. What to Westerners appears as 'control of terrorism' or 'maintaining free trade' bears quite a different aspect from the other side of the prosperity–poverty fence. Actions that, when seen from a Western perspective, seem commonsensically altruistic (or at least neutral) appear riddled with double standards: 'Democracy is promoted but not if it brings Islamic fundamentalism to power'. One thinks of Western acquiescence in the aborting of the Algerian elections and the continuation of the military regime. Furthermore,

> nonproliferation is preached for Iran and Iraq but not
> for Israel; free trade is the elixir of economic growth but
> not for agriculture; human rights are an issue with
> China but not with Saudi Arabia; aggression against oil-
> owning Kuwaitis is massively repulsed but not against
> non-oil-owning Bosnians.[4]

The impatient 'ah, but' responses that most of us (including me) will want to make to such complaints of inconsistency are beside the point here; the point is to see how these 'justifiable' actions by Western powers look very different from a non-Western point of view – that is, from a majority point of view. From that standpoint, the continued exertion of Western power across the world – cultural, economic, military – appears to be transparently self-seeking. 'Human rights' and 'free trade' appear to be no more than mantras that bear no connection with disinterested altruism, let alone with an ethical foreign policy.

And as for Western promises to clean up the mess afterwards . . . ! Reconstruction was promised for Bosnia, but nearly a decade after Dayton the country is still in the deep freeze. It was promised for Serbia after the Kosovo crisis and the fall of Milošević: still nothing. Afghanistan presents, admittedly, a bigger challenge – but don't expect transformation of that country anytime soon. Tony Blair made the most shamelessly unbelievable promises to Macedonia in 2001 that, if the Macedonian government would compromise with its Albanian separatist insurgents and accept NATO peacekeepers, then the country would definitely, oh-but-definitely, be fast-tracked into EU membership; predictably, not a thing has been heard of this promise since.

Violence is an unsurprising response to this predicament, a predicament that is experienced by many non-Westerners as humiliation. Quite obviously, violence is the only way to get the West's attention. What else explains the feverish popularity of Saddam Hussein across the Arab world during the 1991 Gulf War? No one, not even Arabs, could be under any illusions but that Saddam was a brutal, murderous thug. But he was *their* brutal, murderous thug! Any spoke in the wheel of the Western juggernaut will serve. Similarly, few were under any illusions that the invasion of Kuwait by Iraq was a good thing; the opposition was not to the solution proposed by the West, but to the West's ability to impose a solution in 'Arab space' at all.

Islamist movements were on the rise before the end of the Cold War. With the demise of communism, however, their accelerated growth could have been predicted. The appeal of Marxist guerrilla movements across much of the non-Western world from the 1950s to the 1980s had never lain in the nature of the Marxist creed itself. That had been, if anything, a handicap. Those in the know could see that it did not work; those not in the know (mostly Third World peasants) could hardly be expected to understand the full intricacies of its philosophy. The appeal had rested in the nature of antithesis: it was a weapon against the Western juggernaut. By the end of the 1980s, the socialist project was everywhere in ruins. Islamist movements have become the partial inheritors of Marxism's cachet. Obviously, this hardly applies in Latin America. In parts of Asia and sub-Saharan Africa, however, and among urban blacks in the USA itself, it has nevertheless become the ideological vehicle for anti-Westernism.

Terrorism has been called the weapon of the weak; the weak can be relied upon to use such weapons as they have. Terrorism has the advantage of using the West's own distinctive features against it – an open society (to aid infiltration and hiding), instant and full news coverage (to maximize the political effect), a horror of death or of sustaining even small numbers of casualties (resulting from the absence of any deep-rooted sense of transcendence, and also from the sheer comfort of Westerners' lives). After any action, the rule of law can make prosecution difficult, keeps sentencing mild and mostly rules out any kind of blanket retribution (though the attacks on 11 September have put that last point under pressure). Viewed in that light, the man with the truck bomb becomes easier to understand.

## The qualities of barbarism

A number of criteria by which Westerners appear to non-Westerners as barbarous were noted above. These are so contentious that they deserve to be discussed individually.

### No votes for the dead

No society has succeeded in breaking with the past and its own traditions as comprehensively as that of the modern West. Indeed, only in Western ideals is 'breaking with the past' an admirable thing to do. Westerners do not in any sense see themselves as having an obligation to reproduce the ways of their ancestors, or to be faithful to the memory of their forefathers; even to mention such things risks evoking an amused smile. And yet such sensibilities have been all but unanimous in traditional cultures – including our own before the onset of modernity. The Chinese tradition of ancestor worship is not entirely atypical; the medieval European cult of the saints amounted to the same thing. Both represent a willingness to be faithful to the past, and to include the voices – and even the (metaphorical) presence – of the dead in the discussions of the living.

Nowadays, we may visit the grave of a loved one and 'talk to Gran', but we know that we do this primarily for ourselves; the sense of transcendence and of historical continuity with both past and future that could give deeper meaning to such rituals largely eludes us. The sense of specific obligation even to the recent dead, let alone to distant ancestors, is little more than a folk memory.

In the early 1990s, a British schoolgirl in her early teens killed herself. A suicide note explained that she had been mercilessly bullied by a gang of other girls and that she could no longer face life in such circumstances. A senior police officer, interviewed on the radio the following day, explained that the prime concern of his officers and of social workers brought in to the case was in caring for the gang members, who might be distraught by feelings that they were responsible for the girl's death. As he pointed out, his responsibility was not to the dead, for whom he could now do nothing, but to the living.

Only in the West. The example is an extreme one, but for that very reason it illustrates graphically the triumph of sentience over fact. The dead feel nothing; while their relatives' interests are still of some account, the deceased themselves have no interests – or even existence – that we can or should take into account. And as for our long-dead ancestors . . .

## Condescension towards religion

This question of the non-existence of obligations to the dead, of course, touches on the absence of transcendence in Western societies. Most major cultures, although not all, have been underpinned by adherence to a major religion. The West is unusual in having debunked its own and also in rigorously excluding religious issues from public life.

Even more remarkable is the cheerful confidence displayed by most Westerners in the falsity of any 'hard' religious claims. What eighteenth- and nineteenth-century rationalism began, the rise of functional rationality and technocracy have completed.

> As modernisation drives forward, more and more of what was formerly left to God, or human initiative and the processes of nature is classified, calculated and controlled by the use of reason. When reason has harnessed all the facts, figures and forces, divine intervention is as unwelcome as accident, divine law as antiquated as the divine right of kings. Human spontaneity becomes 'the human factor', the weak link in the chain of procedures. Wonder, along with humility and the sanctity of things, is totally out of place. . . . [It] is not that practical reason is irreligious, but that in more and more areas of life religion is practically irrelevant.[5]

As the sociologist David Lyon puts it, 'Acts of Parliament or parking meters will answer all.'[6]

In Western experience, the countries that modernized first were those, such as the UK and the Netherlands, in which leading religious institutions lost the power, during the early modern period, to enforce themselves on the populace, and so granted a limited religious toleration. With the passing of time, the scope of the toleration widened. The rise of the USA (which was founded on the principle of the separation of Church and State) as the pre-eminently modern society compounded the perceived link between modernity and secularization. The Roman Catholic countries of southern Europe modernized more slowly and later, and did so in the teeth of resistance from the Roman Catholic Church. When we remember that the Enlightenment project began, in part, as a reaction against the religious wars of the seventeenth century, and so as a search for a rational, non-religious basis for public policy, it is not hard to see how religion has retreated further and further into the private sphere of the home and personal devotion – if even there.

Tom Paine, writing in 1792, was a little ahead of his time in the vigour with which he expressed the connection between secularism and modernity but, as in so many things, he was a popular herald of intellectual trends and an apologist for modernizing views. Referring to the connection of Church and State, he comments that 'we shall see the ill effects it has had on the prosperity of nations. The union of Church and State has impoverished Spain. Revoking the Edict of Nantes drove the silk manufacture from France into England.' (The Edict of Nantes was a limited permission of toleration to French Huguenots, granted in 1598 and finally revoked by Louis XIV in 1685, thus initiating the persecution of those who remained.) Religion, urged Paine, had no business in public life, for

if everyone is to judge of his own religion, there is no
such thing as a religion that is wrong; but if they are to
judge of each other's religion, there is no such thing as a
religion that is right; and therefore, all the world is
right, or all the world is wrong. But with respect to religion itself, . . . it is man bringing to his Maker the fruits
of his heart . . .

Religion in the West has spent the next two centuries crawl-
ing into the box that Paine opened for it. It remains now a
museum piece, a refuge of 'the heart' but, with respect to
actions in the world, above (or perhaps beneath) rightness
or wrongness, truth or falsehood.[7]

By now it is 'common sense' that religion cannot be a
motivating force in public life. Public metanarratives about
rights and responsibilities, economic requirements, environmental threats and so on must be careful to root themselves
in no deeper soil than that of public utility; they may not
notice the divine. Consequently, even the actions of private
individuals are unlikely to take religious motivations
seriously. Even consciously committed religious believers in
Western countries live highly secularized lives; they do not,
in actual fact, spend nearly as much time in religious devo-
tions, or in hedging their actions and decisions about with
religious criteria and considerations, as does even a very
averagely devout, but non-westernized Muslim in an Islamic
country or a Hindu in India. It is all very embarrassing for
the Christian missionary in the non-West. Religion as a
personal spiritual technique and consolation (like, say,
meditation) survives in the West; religious doctrine as a
guide to action in the world and to the shape of ultimate
reality is considered crazy, even dangerous. If one differs
from this assessment, it is bad taste to do anything other
than keep quiet about it.

When Westerners are confronted with other cultures that
do differ from this Western norm, they are characteristically

struck by a combination of incredulity, embarrassment, amusement and irritation at such 'backwardness'. Convinced by their background that religion is set to die out, yet confronted by powerful evidence to the contrary, 'it is this painful cognitive dissonance . . . that accounts for the peculiar rancour and intolerance' of the irreligious towards the devout.[8] When conflicts break out in the non-West over religious issues – as they frequently do – the Western 'common sense' approach is further confirmed; Westerners themselves would not risk their lives in conflict for anything but personal self-interest (certainly not for abstractions like 'democracy'). This outlook manifests itself in an attitude of condescension towards those of deeply held religious beliefs, a condescension so transparent that it invariably leads to irritation – and worse – on the part of its objects.

## The culture of triviality

The shallowness and triviality of Western culture – for example, its obsession with fashion or with entertainers – is certainly not without its appeal for non-Westerners either. But the spread of such fads to the non-West is perceived as part of the threat to traditional values. The things traditionally prized – wisdom, skills in hunting and riding, religion, honour, the creation of solid or beautiful artefacts – all related directly or indirectly to the business of staying alive and perpetuating the community and its values into the future. By contrast, the obsessions of the West (or of its copycat Third World variants) are connected with appearance and ephemerality and, as often as not, with the commercialization of sex.

The possible benefits to me of consuming a McDonald's hamburger, for example, include my own enjoyment and convenience and (if the country where I live is poor enough to admire such things) the status that I shall attain from haunting such an eating house. I am also identifying myself as a cosmopolitan, whose tastes, aspirations and connections transcend the limits of the purely local. It is the kind of buzz that some Westerners can still experience (though less and less these days) from frequent, especially long-distance, air travel; the kudos that used to be associated with the phrase 'the jet set'. To the traditional world of social stability, solidarity and permanence, this is all anathema. It is not simply a difference in judgement about taste (puns aside), but about the whole meaning of social existence. It is a clash of cultures. McDonald's represents the egocentric, the non-communitarian, the non-traditional, the foreign, the unrestrained, the self-indulgent. It represents the West. That is not to say that it is not desirable, or even tempting – but that is precisely what makes it a problem.

Clearly, the same could be said of fashions in clothing. Or of film-stars. Their very allure threatens to substitute the transitory and the ephemeral for the settled and the solid. To that extent, they are not merely similar to the temptation of drug-taking; they are the same temptation. Like them, they seem to threaten anarchy. Countries that are too poor to be run on democratic lines cannot allow their members the kinds of individualistic freedoms and lifestyle choices that imply democratic values. They have to rest on something more solid.

### Sexual shamelessness
The ability of a run-of-the-mill disco in outer-London suburbia to advertise a weekly 'Lust Night' in an effort to boost attendance illustrates, even more graphically than the sexualized nature of advertising or of fashion clothing, the prevalence of sexual shamelessness.

Sexual immorality is no kind of exclusive preserve of the contemporary West, of course, though perhaps the all-pervasiveness of it is. This all-pervasiveness is part of the reason for the passion with which Westerners reject religious values as any kind of guide to action, or as anything more than a personal spiritual technique. If religion re-emerged from Paine's box, it would start raising truth claims and impinging on our freedom of action in areas such as sexual behaviour.

But any departures from sexual propriety have been accompanied in all traditional societies – even including, for this purpose, the West itself until the mid-twentieth century – by a sense of shame and disgrace which, far more than any formal sanctions, did much to keep such behaviour within bounds. The overall direction of Western culture away from such restrictions has been vastly accelerated by the invention of (mostly) reliable methods of birth control. Campaigners against the dissemination of contraceptives in the early twentieth century argued that it would increase promiscuity; their opponents replied that, on the contrary, it would increase domestic harmony and empower women. Domestic harmony has not noticeably improved since then, at least as measured by the divorce statistics, the sexual bargaining power of women (that is, a woman's ability to make sexual favours conditional upon a man's lifetime commitment to keep her and her offspring) has collapsed, and promiscuity has risen sharply. It is hard not to conclude that the predictions of the 'no' campaigners were correct.

By now, sexual 'freedom' has been elevated to the status of principle in most Western countries. Consequently, it can come as no surprise that Westerners are viewed with the same disdain in this regard that unmarried mothers in the 1960s experienced from the older generation. (Patricia Morgan, in her book *Farewell to the Family?*[9], demonstrates that government welfare and taxation policies in the 1980s and 1990s positively favoured single mothers, to the extent that, in lower income groups, a man in the home was an actual financial encumbrance.) One incident in the mid-1990s illustrates this clash of cultures well. A 13-year-old British girl met a young Turkish waiter while on holiday in Turkey and a romance began. They wished to marry and, with the support of his family and the girl's single mother, did so, at which the British press was scandalized and outraged. Although the Turkish authorities eventually intervened and the relationship broke up, ordinary Muslims were perplexed. Many Western girls indulge in sex at this age, and teenage pregnancies are common; here was a man willing to act, not immorally, but morally, by taking a young girl into the permanent arrangement of marriage. Where was the problem? Did Westerners actually prefer promiscuity? Or was it just another case of anti-Muslim prejudice?

But the differences really did go all the way down to the ground. Sex at the age of 13 was not really the problem for Westerners; if it was, they would make serious efforts in schools, homes and law courts to stop it – but of course they do not. What was really scandalous, to the Western mind, was the foreclosing of future freedoms, at such a young age, by the bond of marriage.

Small wonder that Western women are considered 'an easy touch' in non-Western countries. Small wonder that non-Western men are torn between the desire to sample the forbidden fruit that their contacts with the Western lifestyle offer and the urge to lock up their own womenfolk for fear that they may be contaminated by it.

## Hanging loose to the family

The fragility of families is an obvious corollary of sexual freedom. Sex is what makes families both possible and necessary; if it is not regulated, then the structure of the family will inevitably become rather diffuse.

In prosperous, urbanized economies, such as those of the contemporary West, the unavoidable dependency of older people, children, nursing mothers and pregnant women on the working population can be mediated through bureaucracies, social security systems, public and private pension plans and government schooling. Families, the traditional support network, can afford to fail as the principal mechanism of economic provision. (Whether or not this is really the case, of course, is hotly disputed, but at least prosperous countries can afford to mess around with social experiments on the hypothesis that it is true, without anyone actually starving to death.) In any other kind of society (that is, all traditional societies of the past and in Third World countries today), survival depends on long-lasting relationships with known people, particularly family members.

Consequently, family has been a principal focus of values and devotion in every culture. The very phrase 'filial piety' (seldom used now), reminds us of the *gravitas* that used to be attached to the family bond. To be sure, Western countries retain the lip-service of rhetoric about 'the family', but they do not want to pay the price of restricted freedom on personal actions that any actualization of the rhetoric could imply. 'Family' is a 'sunset value' in the West; the more the reality declines, the more its power as a word that carries emotional connotations increases. So Westerners mostly insist that 'different sorts of family are possible', or 'equally valid', as the favoured phrase goes. ('Valid' with reference to what?) Even the more conservative of Westerners frequently live hundreds of miles from their ageing parents and view them, however affectionately, as an encumbrance.

Idealization of the 'extended families' of the past is as mistaken as avoiding the uncomfortable truths about the present; life under the eye of an aged patriarch (or, more often, matriarch) could be tyrannous. There are parts of the Arab world where mothers-in-law continue to undertake the duties of subjugating their daughters-in-law with all customary relish.

It was the Industrial Revolution that first forced our ancestors to 'get on their bikes' (in Norman Tebbit's phrase) and look for work. Only a minority of them moved far from home at first – mostly no further than the nearest industrial town. But once the first few generations of urbanites had grown up with no continuing family links to the countryside, the anonymity of existence in a large town became the norm. The nuclear family became a self-contained, free-floating social unit in an urban soup of people. It made its own decisions about where to live, what to buy, which job to take and whom to marry, with less and less reference to the concerns or opinions of wider kinfolk. The tyrannous mother-in-law has been replaced by the supplicant old lady, pleading or wheedling for a few chances each year to see her own grandchildren. And in our own time, of course, even the nuclear family has begun to break down.

The very notions of 'going out to work' and, even more, of the middle-class concept of 'pursuing a career' have transformed the nature of the family. Before the Industrial Revolution comparatively few people 'went out to work', and economic production took place in and around the home. The family was itself the unit of economic production. That was – and in the Third World still is – part of the reason why family solidarity was so necessary for survival. It also had the effect of creating much stronger bonds between people. The advent of 'going out to work', however, made the home a unit of consumption, not production; it was where the pay packet was brought back to. The family became primarily a unit of emotional support and consumer spending, divorced from economic output. The world was being divided into public and private realms.

If 'going out to work' increased geographical mobility, 'pursuing a career' accelerated the process. Careers were – and are – for the bourgeois and the professional; by definition, they exclude the unskilled and the labourer. They also need, more often than not, to be pursued over a wide terrain. If the company wants to move you to Yorkshire or Alabama, you had better move. If the firm is too small to provide scope for promotion, you open the trade journal and consult the 'Vacancies' column. With the bourgeoisification of Western societies, especially since the Second World War, life-long association with place has been strangled. Where adherence to place and solidarity of wider kin-groups still carry any weight, it is an almost infallible sign, as in southern Italy, of economic poverty and social backwardness. Unless you are willing to have your horizons limited by the town of your birth, then close association across the generations, and between siblings over a lifetime, will be the exception, not the rule. For Westerners, that is now 'common sense'.

## No question of honour

If most of the values that characterized societies throughout history (and that still characterize non-westernized people) are merely rejected by Westerners, the value of 'honour' is scarcely even understood by them. In the Western mind, an insistence on 'honour' is equivalent to a sort of ludicrous strutting posture adopted by those with little to strut about, like a cock crowing on its own dunghill. We might agree that that such 'honour' is the characteristic of poor societies (though it is certainly not confined to the poor within those societies). Those who have little else can at least have a reputation for honour.

For us in the West, its last echoes are present in the gangster movie or the cowboy film, where the gunman gets the man who killed his brother. It is present in the feud of the *mafiosi* or under the Albanian Kanun of Lek Dukagjin. Apart from such picturesque remnants from Europe's late-developing Sicilian or Balkan margins, however, honour is now the preserve of the non-West.

Honour is about the avoidance of losing face. It is about the battle against shame. But concepts of shame can only have a strong hold where there is an ingrained sense of right and wrong. This is absent from the West, where ethical matters, similarly to religion and choice of career, are held to be subjects of personal preference. If shamelessness is extended to sexual matters, its presence can be more or less taken for granted anywhere else.

To be sure, honour can lead to behaviour that Westerners have long regarded (and probably rightly) as immoral – such as the blood feud. It is associated with pride, with cruelty to women and with showy pretence. However, to the defenders of honour, these are but spiteful names for dignity, chastity and fortitude, values too little regarded in the West. Some aspects of honour are also connected with moral enterprises, such as hospitality, that even a Westerner must admit to be praiseworthy. Most cultures have a tradition of hospitality far more sacrificial than that of Westerners, and it is based on the honour principle: the guest gets the very best, however much it hurts.

## Pots and kettles?

For most Westerners, if charges of 'barbarism' are appropriate language to level at anybody or anything at all, they generally refer to material conditions. Westerners might refer to dirty living accommodation or eating or washing facilities as 'barbarous'. Even more commonly, they might designate cruel treatment of people or animals as 'barbaric'. (Already we can see how quickly the charge of barbarism can be thrown back at some non-Westerners; the mind flashes at once to images of hand amputations, or of female 'circumcision'.)

Such usages certainly have a fair amount of historical justification behind them. The barbaric was understood to be in contrast to that which was urban and literally 'civilized' (meaning rooted in the *civis*, the city); it was the disordered, as opposed to the settled; the crude, rather than the refined. It referred to what was still in a state of nature, as opposed to what had been subjected to human modification and improvement. This kind of use extends back to the Romans, for whom the *barbari* were the bearded ones (or, as we might say, 'the great unwashed') beyond the frontiers of the Empire. It also meant simply 'foreign' or 'strange' – a person who stammered 'bar-bar' in his or her clumsy attempts to speak one's own language.

From that point of view, of course, it could be argued that all cultures are 'barbarous' to all others. Different folk, different folkways; there is nothing further to be said. Yet this would be to miss the point. For in actual practice, and aside from the niceties of etymology, a charge of 'barbarism' contains an actual judgement with wider reference than the mere absolutizing of one's own culture. A barbarian is living or behaving in a way that is unnecessarily brutish or animal-like.

The Romans themselves, it should be remembered, were capable of cruelties all the more extreme and terrifying for being so ruthlessly efficient and organized, whether the mass crucifixions of Spartacus's slave-revolt or of rebellious Jews in Palestine, whether the throwing of criminals and Christians to the lions or the gladiatorial fights to the death before bloodlusty audiences of tens of thousands. The Romans would doubtless have defended themselves against charges of barbarism because *their* violence was so well orchestrated and disciplined, unlike the wild fury of the tribal war-hosts. The Nazis made the same defence of their death-camps. Many of us, it is to be hoped, would beg to differ from so narrow a definition.

It is not intended to take issue with contemporary Western identifications of 'barbarism'. Doubtless they are justified, but the ambiguity in the case of the Romans and their cruelty should remind us that modern Western countries have put a premium on sensibility; for us, 'cruelty' is one of the few crimes that we can still rouse ourselves to condemn. It is not that the condemnation is unjust (for it assuredly is not), but that the infliction of physical or emotional pain is not the only measure of barbarism, any more than a pain-free life is the only good. Cruelty has more power to shock us (whose lives are, after all, more comfortable than those of any other people who have ever lived), and that is probably all to the good. But that sensibility comes at a price. The price is a desensitizing to many other evils that all cultures other than ours have considered to be offensive. That their offensiveness eludes us is no small measure of our own barbarism.

The ordinary, everyday experience of most of the people who have ever lived – frequent exposure to cold and wet; infrequent washing; the need to kill, skin and clean one's own dinners; strong and unpleasant smells; expectations of high infant mortality; the need to handle dead bodies; chronic and untreatable illness and pain; short life expectancy – looks harsh and cruel enough to the eyes of a pampered, modern or post-modern Westerner. In traditional societies, any sanctions against miscreants and any firm treatments of others start with that (to us) harsh enough experience of every day as a baseline. Any rough treatment or punishment that *is* a punishment will, by definition, have to be harsher than that. That does not in any way excuse witch-burning, or the 'death of ten thousand cuts', or female circumcision. But it does signal to us that most cultures – and individuals – have had 'tolerance levels' of physical harshness and cruelty (that is, in inflicting it and in witness-ing it) that exceed our own. Cruelty has been condemned by all cultures, but it is not surprising if, in most cases, the far ends of the spectra of permissibility jut out consistently well beyond ours.

We can insist, if we will, on our own canons of what constitutes 'barbarism': cruelty as measured by distance from our own unique comforts; restrictions on behaviour as contrasted with the freedoms made possible by our own superabundant wealth; social distinction as measured against our own atomized individualism and egalitarianism. But then we shall find that we have excommunicated all cul-tures but our own, as well as our own past. We may decide not to shrink even from that move, of course, but then we cannot simultaneously continue to insist that we are being tolerant and (dammit) multicultural. By absolutizing the unique – not to say historically aberrant – culture of the post-Enlightenment West, we have become the ultimate cultural imperialists. And then we wonder why we're hated.

# On the importance of being earnest

When the Protestant reformers of the sixteenth century complained about the legalism of the Roman Church, they were making a decisive break, not merely with late-medieval religion, but with traditional ways of talking and thinking about morality – as found not just in the pre-modern West but also in the non-West. The codes of morality that have upheld social order and fended off primal chaos throughout history, from Cathay to the Congo and from Cuzco to Catalonia, have all emphasized external acts: those things that are to be done and those things that are not to be done. In most religious codes, salvation (or a better karma next time around) were accorded to those who did well, and damnation (or perhaps reincarnation as a slug) to those who did not.

### Shift number 1: from 'fending off chaos' to 'integrity'

Martin Luther's protest against this way of thinking was the result of his testing the system to the limits and finding himself an incorrigible sinner despite his very best efforts. Perhaps no one in history has tried harder than Luther to save his or her own soul. Yet he found that external acts and omissions were only the beginning of the moral calculus; by the time one had taken into account the sinful thoughts, attitudes and motivations that entangle us, none could account themselves excused before an awesome, holy and perfect God who will judge sinners. So at the end of countless penances, visiting of relics, confessions, vigils and good deeds he concluded that he was, nevertheless, damned. The pardons offered by the Church for this or that sin, or for this or that amount of guilt, or to remit such-and-such a period in purgatory, could never be enough. The human being was sinful in every part: 'in my flesh . . . dwelleth no good thing.'[1]

The problem, taught Luther, was our unavoidable lack of integrity: even if we could conform outwardly to the demands of the moral law as taught by the Church (or indeed, to any conceivable moral law), the gulf between that external behaviour, on the one hand, and the inner morass of the thought world and mixed-motive intentionality, on the other, left us all condemned. Jesus had fingered the same problem 1500 years before: 'You have heard that it was said, "Do not commit adultery". But I tell you that anyone who looks at a woman lustfully has already committed adultery with her in his heart.'[2] On this set of scales, all of us are adulterers.

The solution, Luther argued, was to abandon hope in oneself and one's own efforts, and to trust in Christ's sacrifice on behalf of sins and in his resurrection as a guarantee to the believing soul of deliverance from eternal death. For the believer, the fear and anxiety generated by dues-paying morality could be left behind, because he or she was justified by the merits of another, namely Christ.

The objection to this hypothesis was obvious, and so the furore created by Luther's theological analysis was entirely predictable: if people believe that they are justified by faith, irrespective of the merits or demerits of their actual behaviour, then moral standards will collapse. For why should they continue to strive to live well? In consequence, the social function of religion, namely its ability to maintain order among the population without constant resort to force, would be fatally undermined.

To this, the various Protestant reformers' riposte was less than entirely convincing. True believers, they assured the doubting authorities of Church and State, would be so grateful to God for the amazing gift of his saving grace that they would live better lives after their conversions than before. Indeed, a transformed life was a sign that one was among the elect.

The trouble with this argument, of course, was that it failed to answer the question of what would happen to those who did not feel themselves to be the recipients of saving grace or who made no pretensions to be among the elect. How would *they* be kept in order? Luther himself vacillated between frank admissions that 'Life among us [namely, in Protestant Wittenberg] is as bad as among the papists' and a reversion to 'the law' for upholding social order:

> We ought to proclaim the law and its works, not for
> Christians, but for the crude and unbelieving. . . .
> Among the crude masses, on Mr Everyman, we must
> use it bodily and roughly . . . Thus they are compelled
> by sword and law to be outwardly pious, much in the
> manner in which we control wild animals with chains
> and pens, so that external peace will exist among the
> people.[3]

Since his theology provided no mechanism for distinguishing between 'the crude masses' and genuine Christians, it remained far from clear how the Reformation, with its doctrines of justification by faith, would save the saints from being treated in exactly the same way as the unconverted. Indeed, it did not. That was the reason many secular authorities stifled their doubts and introduced Protestantism. (Indeed, Augustinian 'invisible church' doctrines and

Luther's own urging that all should be compelled to be 'out-wardly pious' were designed precisely to postpone, from the here-and-now until the *eschaton*, any possibility of making such distinctions between the saved and the damned. In this, all of the magisterial (i.e. State–Church) Protestant reform-ers concurred. It was absolutely essential if any secular authorities at all were to be persuaded to accept the Reformation.)

But what the Reformation did achieve was a long-term stress on the idea of integrity and inwardness that has become a leading feature of Western culture and that remains long after the religious motives that thrust it to prominence have been discarded by an ever more secular society. Its diffused, secularized form has become the inher-itance even of the historically Roman Catholic regions of the West, so that it is today a key differentiation between 'the West and the rest'. This originally Protestant insight, which saturated popular consciousness in those countries that embraced the Reformation, was that outward behav-iour was not enough – there was an inner self which God sees.

For the reformers themselves, of course, the primary point of this insight was to stress the depth of our sinfulness and need of a Saviour – we could not be justified by our outward works, for our inner motives and thoughts were confounded. However, their *secondary* point, namely that our inner world should ideally be brought into harmony with our outward behaviour (as part of the process of sanc-tification), became, in popular consciousness, the *primary* point: the Reformation put a premium on honesty, integrity and plain dealing – that is, on harmony between the inner and outer man.

It was this aspect, of course, that was so conducive to the emerging commercial culture of the sixteenth and seven-teenth centuries. 'My business' may perhaps grow rich by sharp practices, but for business in general to thrive a culture of trust is necessary. Integrity was, in that sense, a supremely pragmatic virtue. By the nineteenth century, 'an Englishman's word is his bond' was an axiom that helped to make England the richest country in the world.

Far from accidentally, it was the Anglo-Saxons upon whom the thought world of the Bible had made the deepest impression, and whose language remains, more than any other, deeply infected with biblical and quasi-biblical turns of phrase ('the right hand doesn't know what the left hand is doing', 'the sheep and the goats', 'keeping on the straight and narrow', 'being all things to all men', 'washing one's hands of something'). Such phrases are used unreflectively, long after the conscious rejection of their Christian origins. This is not to argue that no inhabitants of Roman Catholic or Eastern Orthodox Europe paid any attention to interiority – clearly many did so, both before the Reformation and afterwards. But we are concerned here, not with the few, but with the many; not with the conspicuous saints, but with the maybe-not-even-converted; not with intellectuals *qua* intellectuals, but only with the real – and almost always long-delayed – effects of their ideas at the grass roots. And it was Protestant culture that nurtured the idea that, when you gave to the poor, your right hand shouldn't know what your left hand was doing – that what mattered was the giving, not the public adulation that might accompany it. And attitudes towards prayer were to be the same: 'Then your Father, who sees what is done in secret, will reward you.'[4] Admonitions to nineteenth-century public school-boys about 'sportsmanship' and 'playing the game' are only superficially secular; they could have originated nowhere but in a Protestant country that emphasized purity of motive, of disposition and of the inner person.

This was the first shift – from an emphasis on external behaviour ('works of the law' in Christian parlance) to an emphasis on integrity (a by-product of Protestant doctrines of sin and the consequent highlighting of interiority).

It represented a significant moral gain. By highlighting the need for honesty and integrity, it advanced the causes of both business (and therefore of rising living standards) and, in the long run, political freedoms – for, as Edmund Burke sagely observed,

> Men are qualified for civil liberty in exact proportion to their disposition to put moral chains upon their own appetites . . . Society cannot exist unless a controlling power upon will and appetite be placed somewhere, and the less of it there is within, the more there must be without.[5]

By the nineteenth century, the 'controlling power' within had become strong enough to dispense with many political and social constraints. The internal policeman made his external counterpart redundant. In consequence, Victorian Britain and America could permit the kind of political freedoms that were, quite literally, the envy of other nations, whose refugees flocked there. Yet it is no accident that the high tide of evangelicalism in Victorian Britain created a cultural backwash over succeeding generations which saw crime rates and illegitimacy fall – in circumstances (rapid industrialization and urbanization, a fast-growing population) in which all sociological predictors would have suggested a sharp rise. Indeed, the social historian Gertrude Himmelfarb has shown that crime and illegitimacy (reliable indicators of wider social and moral attitudes) fell, not merely proportionately, but absolutely, during the period from the 1840s to 1901.[6] The graphs in her book show figures proportionate to population, and these indicate sharp falls on both counts. However, when the population figures for 1841 and 1901 (26.85 million and 41.6 million, respectively) are taken into account, then a small reduction even in the absolute figures can be deduced – a quite astonishing fact.

## Shift number 2: from 'integrity' to 'being true to oneself'

However, by the beginning of the twentieth century a second shift in moral dynamic was already starting to take effect – one that would unravel the moral gains of the first. The stress on interiority was heightened, such that it broke loose from its bearings to the moral law and became its own focus. The psalmist's 'Truth in the inner parts . . . wisdom in the inmost place' gave way to Shakespeare's 'To thine own self be true'.[7] And 'being true to oneself' was to become an ever more powerful idea during the course of the twentieth century. (An Internet trawl on the phrase 'To thine own self be true' unearths all manner of self-awareness, therapeutic and otherwise 'New Agey' websites. To this injunction, Luther would presumably have responded, as he did to the Occamists, '*Homo quando facit quod in se est, peccat*' – 'The man who does "that which in him lies" sins'.[8]) 'Integrity' has slowly ceased to mean primarily a conformity of the inward person to outward morality; instead, it has come to mean a congruity between the inner and outer person regardless of the actual content of that individual's beliefs, morals or ideals.

Thus by the late twentieth century, people who were quite promiscuous in their behaviour but upheld 'sexual freedom' as an ideal (and were not such a 'humbug' as to do otherwise) would count as people of 'integrity'; they were, after all, being 'true to themselves'.

This second shift is largely a result of the growing (and continuing) effects of Romanticism. The first shift had created awareness of a non-idealized, sinful self, upon the appetites of which each person must put 'chains', in the interests of real, rather than superficial, morality. On that earlier view, the self had meaning only by reference to the fixed points of morality to which it might, or might not, conform. The second shift, by contrast, idealizes the self and discards all notion of external fixed points. The first shift had radicalized traditional morality by internalizing it; the second shift radicalizes interiority and discards traditional morality.

Because stress upon interiority had for long been part and parcel of moral discourse under the first shift, it was possible for advocates of the second shift to borrow its language and to sound more 'moral' than those who opposed them (because they were more 'honest', less 'hypocritical' and so on) – even as they cut loose from morality as traditionally understood. In the Romantic worldview of Jean-Jacques Rousseau, the individual is intrinsically good whereas society is evil. For him, there is no question of people needing to put 'chains upon their own appetites', but rather to break the fetters that society imposes upon individuals: 'Man was born free, but he is everywhere in chains'.[9] It is society that drags people down into badness; so the way to better people is by freeing them from the 'chains' of social constraints – and letting them be 'true to themselves'. By the start of the twentieth century, such thinking had spread beyond the narrow circle of intellectuals and been absorbed by the wider middle classes; it was beginning to affect popular thinking about morality.

To be sure, notions of 'integrity' and remnants of its earlier content linger in the ex-Protestant West, even today. People in the UK, the USA and the Netherlands still find themselves bemused by the consistently perfidious dealings of business contacts in the non-West. They are similarly astonished to find that ducking and weaving around regulations and laws is not, as it might be in their own case, a conscious decision for immorality or illegality in some particular circumstance. Rather, it is instinctive behaviour and a ubiquitous tendency in all circumstances. After all, in the pre-modern mind-set that still obtains in much of the non-West, outward conformity to the rules is all that counts.

The ancestors of the present-day British, the colonial

administrators of the late nineteenth century who inhabited the world of the first shift but not of the second, sensed all of this much more strongly. For them, the 'natives' over whom they ruled were 'tricky' and untrustworthy – and those judgements were not rooted entirely in cultural myopia. By contrast, today's Western inhabitants of the second shift are a little less judgemental towards non-Westerners but equally – perhaps more – uncomprehending: people have a right to act in any way they want, it is now reasoned, but why should they profess a morality, or principles, to which they do not wholeheartedly adhere behind closed doors?

But overall, the results of the second shift have transferred any feelings of moral superiority from Westerners to non-Westerners. The latter do at least adhere to traditional morality – in principle, if not always in practice. Postmodern Westerners do no such thing. Thus they appear as barbarians to many of the inhabitants of the Middle East and Asia, whose relative economic and political powerlessness is rendered all the more intolerable to them in consequence.

## In praise of hypocrisy

For post-modern people, the two big sticks with which to beat the morality of their ancestors are those of 'oppression' and 'hypocrisy'. Traditional morality is perceived as having been oppressive in the sense that it prevented individual people from 'being themselves'. The pre-modern, traditional outlook minimized the importance – or at least the autonomy – of self-hood altogether; the first-shift, Reformation legacy depicted the self as sinful and thus in need of putting 'chains' on its appetites, both for its own good and for the welfare of society. But it is Romanticism whose eighteenth-century intellectual origins came to high tide in late modernity and informed the second shift, in which the self is idealized; anything extrinsic that hinders the 'free development' of the individual – such as the constraints imposed by traditional morality – must therefore be evil and oppressive.

The second big stick with which to beat traditional morality is that of 'hypocrisy'. And hypocritical behaviour is uniformly identified as the cardinal sin of the Victorians. Whenever I ask a class of students what vice they most associate with the Victorian era, 'hypocrisy' is the first answer I get. Conversely, whenever I ask with which society or period they most associate the word 'hypocrisy', someone will quickly volunteer 'the Victorians'. Outside my seminary lecture room (and occasionally even inside it), anyone today voicing the opinion that Western society should return to 'Victorian values' – or even moderate its narcissism and hedonism – is likely to be castigated as a hypocrite, or else of wishing society to revert to Victorian moral hypocrisy.

It is worth asking why this should be so. What exactly is hypocrisy, and why do we associate it with Victorianism?

Clearly, to be a hypocrite is to be two-faced in one's moral life; hypocrisy is human badness, observing human goodness and feigning to be like it. The only motive for such behaviour is the fear (experienced by those who act badly) of the disapprobation that they will experience if seen in their true colours, or (what is the same thing) a desire for the social approval that rewards those who do – or seem to do – right. It is, in a word, the very antithesis of integrity.

As such, the temptation to hypocrisy will be greatest in those societies where popular support for morality and integrity are at their strongest. This circumstance precisely describes the Victorian era. Evangelicalism was at its apogee, on both sides of the Atlantic, in the mid-nineteenth century. Protestantism had already shaped the mind-set of the Anglo-Saxons for several centuries. The Great Awakening of the eighteenth century had then intensified the effects of the cult of 'integrity', with its deep, passionate inwardness, but only in the minority of the population who had been affected by it. By the early nineteenth century, however, that minority was becoming sizeable. The 'reformation of manners' was proceeding apace in the wake of sustained evangelical (especially Methodist) growth. The process is most simply illustrated by comparing, in the portraiture of the time, the necklines of high-society ladies in the age of Jane Austen and the Napoleonic wars with those obtaining in the 1850s. The former left little to the imagination; the latter left nothing to be seen.

The statistics of the expansion of evangelical nonconformity during that period speak for themselves, while the evangelical party within the Church of England grew from its nadir in the early eighteenth century to become vociferous and influential at every level of society by the time of Victoria's accession to the throne in 1837. There was never a time when the majority of the population was converted. But, by the mid-nineteenth century, those who had not been knew, by and large, that they should be. Above all, they knew that they should behave in a Christian manner and allow their lives and attitudes to be imbued with a Christian-informed conscience. Otherwise, what else was John Stuart Mill protesting against?

This was the social scenario that produced the falling crime and illegitimacy rates to which Gertrude Himmelfarb points – social trends that continued for at least two generations after the explicitly religious beliefs that underpinned them had started to decline – until, like an overhanging rock whose defiance of gravity could no longer be sustained in the wake of the long, continuous and far-advanced erosion of the cliffs and beach beneath, the 'moral overhang' of Victorian Britain tottered in the 1920s and finally collapsed in the 1960s.

From the 1960s certainly (and in reality long before), there was no more need for hypocrisy. For hypocrisy can only subsist in societies that uphold 'the good' – a good to which sinful human beings cannot fully and consistently attain. And the more enthusiastically and successfully 'the good' is upheld and observed, the more hypocrisy is necessary as a cover for those who do not achieve it (which will be some people all of the time and all people some of the time). Thus the Victorian age, which most strongly upheld – and produced – moral integrity, also, by the same token, produced its converse, hypocrisy.

We need not rub our eyes. All societies set some particular value at a premium and, in doing so, produce its opposite as an inevitable by-product. The value that is put at a premium by a culture will be that which is most necessary to sustain it, that which holds at bay its deepest fear and gravest danger. And by prioritizing it, and thereby working against human (sinful) nature, the imperfect human material will inevitably buckle somewhere, and so produce, sometimes but not all of the time, the very antithesis of what is desired.

In pre-modern societies (that is, societies whose ethics have not accepted either the first or the second shifts we have been discussing here), the premium was – and is – order and freedom from anarchy. Pre-modern societies are, by definition, closest to a state of nature; they consist of people barely subsisting from one year (or sometimes from one day) to the next. In such circumstances, the temptations to resort to force against one's fellows are very strong. Hence the deepest fear of such societies is represented by violence and disorder. Pre-modern morality, therefore, is about keeping at bay the primal forces of chaos. Obedience is its cardinal virtue.

The net result is both success (pre-modern societies are, typically, hideously constricting of behaviour and hierarchical in structure, and they look with ill favour on individual enterprise and initiative) and failure (serious collapses in law and order, at least at the local level, are both more frequent and far more lethal in pre-modern, or Third World, societies than in modern ones).

The late-modern West, by contrast, came to place a premium on freedom and individual selfhood – a self to which one must be 'true'. In this it has been, like pre-modern societies, both spectacularly successful (never before on earth have individuals enjoyed so much freedom to invent and re-invent their lives, or to determine their own meanings for those lives) – and utterly disastrous (nowhere else has there been such a prevalence of schizophrenia and other mental illnesses, such a craving for 'self-esteem', such symptoms of self-loathing as anorexia and self-harm, such a fractured sense of self experienced even by people who appear to 'have it together'). The post-modern trend is to conclude, in the light of the failures, that there is no 'real me' to whom I must be 'true'; instead, there is only superficiality, artifice and appearance.

So, it should come as no surprise that the society which most successfully put a premium on moral integrity (that is, Victorian society) was also characterized by its converse, namely hypocrisy.

Hypocritical behaviour is, of course, a bad thing – but the existence of the phenomenon is a sign of a good thing. One can only be guilty of it if one aspires (or at least feels one ought to aspire) to high moral standards. That is the reason that post-modern Westerners are seldom guilty of this failing. It is also why they castigate it, with such a sense of serene assurance, in the Victorians, or in any today, such as Christians, who are rash enough to espouse an undoing of the sexual revolution of the 1960s. Post-modern people can hardly be guilty of hypocrisy (that is, of failing to live up to high moral standards while pretending to do so), for they make no pretence of espousing traditional morality in the first place.

When Jesus denounced hypocrisy in the Pharisees, he did so while speaking to an audience who believed, as he did, in traditional moral codes in their full rigour. He called on his followers to be above hypocrisy. If post-modern people are guiltless of this failing, however, it is not because they are above hypocrisy, but because they are beneath it. Without in the least detracting from Jesus' denunciations of Pharisaic moral double-dealing, I would venture to suggest that our circumstance is one that the Gospel writers – indeed, any pre-modern source – did not entirely envisage. To be guilty of hypocrisy, one has first to accept the validity of the morals on which it is predicated – and our culture, uniquely, does not.

If Christians wish to call, therefore, for a return to both the public espousal and the private practice of traditional morality, they need to confront the fact that 'hypocrisy' will be an occupational hazard of the journey. We need to work, not for hypocrisy (obviously), but for a situation in which the crime of the hypocrite is once again possible. The propaganda of our age notwithstanding, there are fates, and conditions, even worse than hypocrisy. Moral anomie is one of them.

# How to be sinless: human rights and the death of obligations

Human rights have increasingly become the defining idea in Western morality over the past two centuries. They have changed our concepts of right and wrong and of permissibility and impermissibility. At least as importantly, they have changed the very nature of moral debate.

It bears repeating, therefore, that human rights are essentially an invention of the eighteenth-century Enlightenment. Traditional systems of morality worked on the principle of obligation: act thus, don't do that, you must, you ought not. Human rights reverse this, and tell the person what is his or her due. The person from whom something was expected becomes instead the putative recipient of care or provision, with hand outstretched in righteous demand.

## 'Hath God said?': the death of the will of God

The circumstances of the birth of 'human rights' relate to the debunking of revealed religion by the philosophers and intellectuals of the Enlightenment. Revealed religion had been the source of endless quarrels in western and central Europe during the sixteenth and seventeenth centuries, culminating in the horrors of the Thirty Years War (1618–48), during which the German-speaking lands suffered the loss of a larger proportion of their populations than they were to do in the Second World War. The death rate in Bohemia and Moravia (partly German-speaking then) may have been as high as 50 per cent in some districts. The various countries of the British Isles had also been torn apart by their own Civil Wars during the 1640s and 1650s. That fighting, although it had not been caused directly by religious differences, nevertheless took on the nature – and sometimes the viciousness – of religious warfare, especially during the later stages of conflict. As Oliver Cromwell sagely expressed it, 'Religion was not the thing at first contended for, but God brought it to that at the last.' At the end of it all, many English people, like their continental counterparts, felt that they could do without it. Religion did not wither away, but the religious revivals of the eighteenth century were predominantly pietistic; that is, they stressed inward religion and did not make overt bids for political power or call for the persecution of their rivals. The period from the late seventeenth century onwards was characterized by attempts at locating the basis for polity in reason, rather than in quarrelling about differing understandings of the will of God.

Perhaps somewhat contradictorily, this process tended to be more advanced in Protestant countries than in Roman Catholic ones. The Roman Catholic monarchies of Europe mostly tried, after the fighting was over, to shut up shop and make Roman Catholicism a tool of state, not in directing foreign policy or furthering the Counter-Reformation abroad, but in keeping social order and in suppressing 'heresy' at home. Protestant monarchs tried the same, but as often as not theirs was an ill-defined Protestantism-and-water; its God required little more than acknowledgement and an obedience fully encompassed by deference to social superiors and conformity to the law of the land.

The actions of the Roman Catholic states guaranteed two things: that they would, in the long term, become intellectual and scientific backwaters, and that such thinkers and writers as they did produce would be alienated from religion. The tepidity of the Church of England, by contrast, made such heroic repudiations almost unnecessary in England; rationalism made its home within the embrace of the establishment. Either way, the same result: most of the leading philosophers inclined towards deism. Briefly stated, this is the belief that the universe is like a letter that has been dictated but not signed; the existence of a creator may justly be inferred from the evidence of our eyes, but this god is the philosopher's god, the necessary first cause, not a cosmic lawgiver or a being from whom seers and mystics can impart reliable communications.

Accordingly, the thinkers of the eighteenth century sought other grounds than the text of the Hebrew and Christian Scriptures for their moral framework. But if not there, then where? For all practical purposes, deism was tantamount to atheism. To be sure, there was a god, but a god whose only purpose was to exist, by way of an answer to the very reasonable question 'whence all this?'. If one sought practical information, such as the nature of morality and what was to be done, then one must begin, not with an unknowable god, but with ourselves.

Morality, then, does not come to us as a series of commands from on high, or from outside human society at all. It emanates outwards from the human person, with his or her needs. It does not consist of duties, therefore, but of rights.

It was postulated that people first came together, from out of a state of nature, to form societies on the basis of mutual assurances of advantage. Only on the basis of such advantages could any society – or what was more to the point, any government – justify its existence. This fitted in well with the overthrow of tradition and the rejection of governments based on traditional or hereditary claims, such as monarchies. Radicals such as Tom Paine could fulminate against George III, the descendant of 'a Norman bastard and his armed *banditti*', but the real pinch of critiques of this kind was felt most keenly by those European monarchs who still made claims to absolutist governing powers based upon 'the divine right of kings'. Nowhere was this tension greater than in France.

Denis Diderot (1713–84) posited the existence of a 'natural law', which 'would not change because it will always be relative to the general will and the common wishes of the whole species'. As one modern commentator on Diderot observes, 'Of course the ultimate criterion of this code of nature is happiness.'[1] Any restraint on human desires, then, could be justified, not by reference to an unknowable greater happiness in a scarcely imaginable hereafter, but only in the interests of a calculable greater happiness in the here-and-now. Morality was a higher form of pragmatism.

If Christian revelation was now considered a poor basis for morality, there had been many other societies in human history that had not accepted Christian Scripture – or even known of it – and whose moral ideas eighteenth-century thinkers might, in theory, have wished to borrow. Unfortunately, however, non-European societies were held to be inherently inferior; that was why they were in the process of subjugation by Europeans. Furthermore, the moral life of many of them rested upon religious foundations that also laid claim to being 'revealed'. For these reasons, the other great moral traditions that, like the Judaeo-Christian ethic, emphasized obligation and duty rather than rights were disqualified as being equally repressive.

One of the few external inspirations that was an exception to this trend and did influence Enlightenment thinking was an idea projected *on* the non-West, rather than derived *from* it: that of the 'noble savage'. This piece of sheer romanticism expressed the belief that human beings in their 'natural' state were the moral superiors of civilized people. Civilization was held to be corrupting, because all thitherto existing government was corrupt, being based on the notion that people were inherently bad and so in need of laws to restrain their wickedness. According to the new idealists, however, the emphasis on human corruption was a cover for the power of kings and other despots, and was used to justify their control. As Helvétius (1715–71) put it, 'The thing to complain of is not the wickedness of men, but the ignorance of lawmakers.'[2] The true hypothesis, according to rationalists and romantics alike, was that people are actually good; indeed, they are the measure of what constitutes 'good'. If left to themselves, like the noble savage on his island paradise, they would be happier and more moral.

Accordingly, the purpose of laws was not so much to restrain evil as to promote happiness. Noble savages came together to form societies only for the purpose of promoting their mutual welfare, not in order to reduce one another's freedoms. Once again rights, not obligations, were indicated.

By the phrase 'the ignorance of lawmakers', Helvétius had meant not some kind of inevitable ignorance of any conceivable lawmakers in the face of intractable problems or inscrutable questions, but rather the stupidity of actual lawmakers, a stupidity that should be contrasted with the enlightenment of . . . well, of men such as himself. If know-how was the central prerequisite for attaining good governance, then it followed that all problems were, in principle, soluble. Government needed to be wrested from the hands of the self-interested and the ignorant. Their self-justificatory appeals to tradition and religion should be dismissed as so much obscurantist mumbo-jumbo. Power should be delivered into the hands of the people – or rather, into the hands of the *illuminati* who spoke for the people and would give them their rights. The Western belief in human rights, then, has been accompanied, especially in its later, twentieth-century manifestations, by a taken-for-granted certainty that government holds the key to human happiness. Poverty, a sluggish economy, vicious spouses, high crime rates, education, health, the vicissitudes of life: none is beyond the compass of wise legislation.

These, of course, are delusions that political leaders have continued to foster – at least when they are in opposition. By beating present governments with these sticks and insisting that our rulers are, like the absolutist princelings of old, ignorant and self-seeking (never mind the fact that we freely elected them only a couple of years ago!), opposition politicians can stress their own democratic credentials as *vox populi* and as disinterested public servants. They can also promise the moon – for the moon is, after all, deliverable by the government that truly knows how!

All things considered, therefore, it is none too surprising that the nineteenth and twentieth centuries have seen the rise of both utopian creeds and naive democracies. These have varied greatly among themselves – nationalism and fascism, socialism and communism, liberalism, welfarism and free trade – but their unifying thread is that the responsibility for public well-being lies with government, which will give the citizenry those 'rights' of which previous regimes have somehow cheated it.

As responsibilities pile up on an amorphous, impersonal 'them' – the 'system' – so they shift progressively away from the individuals – everyone in society – who go to make up that collectivity. The end result is a society in which no one is to blame for anything, for that would be (horror of horrors!) 'a culture of blame'. Instead, impersonal entities such as government and social arrangements ('the system') are to blame for everything. All problems have solutions and those solutions are political or technocratic.

In this climate, the traditional needs for self-restraint and the acceptance of responsibility for one's own actions are likely, in the long term at least, to wither to the merest vestige. If impersonal systems and structures are to blame for all problems, it follows that any guilt attaching to persons will be the consequence, not of what one does, but of what one is: prosperous maybe, or intelligent, or beautiful. For it is the poor, the ill-educated or unintelligent and unappealing who are aggrieved. If there is any guilt accruing to persons at all, it must be to the beneficiaries of existing conditions or (what must surely be the same thing) supporters of the status quo. One's own dissatisfactions cannot be one's fault, nor can they be the result of natural limitations, either in the self or in the very nature of things or of people. They are the fault of 'society', of laws and procedures that could – and should – have been better, where 'better' is defined as a general state of affairs that does not leave anyone in a less advantageous position than anyone else.

Since no society can sustain itself on such a basis (and not even communism did so, not even nearly), it is consequently very difficult for any social institutions in the West to defend their legitimacy. All of them are in perpetual danger of being debunked by those who can (or, at any rate, who will) claim a grievance against existing arrangements and adopt a righteous posture of 'rights withheld'. Government and electoral systems, family arrangements, structures of taxation, education systems: all live on a perpetual knife-edge of reform or revolution at the hands of those who claim to be disempowered. The only things that are invulnerable are those things that never claimed objective value, such as entertainment and fashion, which are taken with unprecedented seriousness and are at the heart of the infantilization of Western culture.

## The rise and rise of human rights

Human rights began in the eighteenth century as a basis for considering political arrangements. In that sense, they were a tentative extension of the limited idea of rights that had always existed before, namely the legal right to x, y or z as expressed in a given code of law. The Old Testament had spoken of 'the rights of the poor', but this had always been a reference to their legal rights enshrined in the Torah. Similarly, a pre-Enlightenment European could speak of his 'right' to his property, but that was a reference to the actual law of the land; it meant that he had the title deed in his pocket. Where human rights were novel was in speaking of 'right' as an abstract moral principle that may or (more likely) may not be reflected in existing legal conditions. To say that the people had a 'right' to choose their sovereign did not imply that all households had the vote; it meant that they ought to have it. It meant that reason could be used in a way that had the effect of debunking the claims of those presently in authority and of speculating about early human societies and noble savages in such a way that made democracy seem the only moral polity. It meant that 'justice' could be used as an abstraction, divorced from actual juridical codes, and made to appear on the side of those for whom 'rights' were being claimed.

Such argumentation was highly successful. The American and French Revolutions were founded upon the idea of human rights. The former appealed to a vague religiosity: 'the Laws of Nature and of Nature's God'; 'endowed by their Creator'; 'Life, Liberty and the pursuit of Happiness'. The latter was aggressively secularist. With the massive social advances in health and education, and the widespread political emancipation, that were witnessed in the most advanced industrial economies during the nineteenth century, the way was cleared for talk about rights to become increasingly blurred. Once each new legal right had been in place for a generation or more, so that it seemed to be part of the natural order of things, it was easy to speak of it as a 'right' in the looser moral sense. In the late twentieth century, it was perfectly possible to speak of having a 'right' to education – in a manner that implied a moral meaning rather than an empirical or legal one – without being derided as a fool. Well before the end of the twentieth century, any number of items on personal or group wish-lists could be described as 'rights' without any sense of irony or absurdity. The transition was complete.

At least some eighteenth-century observers had sensed the danger. Malouet, a French royalist, had warned the Estates General in 1789: 'Take care when you tell man his rights. For you will thus transport him to the summit of a high mountain – from where you show him an empire without limits.'[3] By the end of the twentieth century this possibility had been fully realized among the wealthiest one-tenth of the global population. While the more westernized inhabitants of Third World and post-communist countries struggled for the kind of rights envisaged by the eighteenth-century luminaries – freedom of speech, the vote, freedom of religion – their First World counterparts had become self-indulgent babies, insisting that the material benefits that only a tiny minority of hyper-prosperous economies had been able to provide in the last generation (and none before that) were somehow intrinsic 'rights' for all people every-where. Indeed, the 'limitless empire' foreseen by Malouet was now challenging the limitations of nature itself – the right to have sex with no consequences (contraception and abortion); the right to have a child without a spouse, or after the menopause, or within a same-sex partnership; the right to be protected from the consequences of one's actions on the grounds of one's (real or alleged) disadvantages: all had become generally accepted.

The sentence beginning 'I have a right to' has become, more often than not, a cover for 'I want' dressed up in a tuxedo and palming itself off as a moral claim – with the distressing concomitant that neither speaker nor listener is generally aware of the transvestism entailed, so thoroughly has 'rights' language become the common currency of moral discourse, resorted to unreflectively by people of all political, moral and religious persuasions.

## *Bi-polar morality*

The logic of rights need not necessarily be used to maximize individual freedoms, of course. Even today, nationalists in eastern Europe stress the idea of 'collective rights', by which they mean the freedom of a majority ethnicity or religion to express itself through the levers of state power and to suppress – or at least to restrict – minorities and dissenters.[4] If such argumentation looks highly suspect to most of those who believe in human rights today, that is because, in the West at least, the individualistic understanding has won out.

It is worth remembering that political life in most Western countries has been dominated by two-party systems which have used the binary logic of 'freedom of the individual' versus 'best for everyone' with relentless force. Centre-right forces have generally been coalitions of economic liberals (espousing individualistic freedoms in the economic arena) and social collectivists (upholding traditional morality and family values in the interests of social cohesion). Centre-left and left-wing parties, on the other hand, have been counter-coalitions of those who favour economic collectivism (restricting free markets in favour of 'social justice') and, at least since the rise of the hippie generation and the *soixante-huitaires*, libertarianism in respect of social relations. Those who espouse feminism or homosexual rights, for example, have found their most natural home on the political Left.

In consequence, all political and moral arguments have tended to take on the nature of a contest between those who wish to maximize individual freedoms and those who wish to do 'what is best for everyone'. In the face of this kind of moral discourse, all intermediate institutions – that is, those that are bigger than the individual but smaller than the 'all' – have found themselves defenceless. The rural community, the minority language and culture, the church, the small school: all of them restrict personal freedoms or the optimization of individual goals. Village communities are nosy; churches are censorious. The Welsh-language community is a small pool in which to make a big splash if one wants a career rather than just a job. The intermediate units are also economically inefficient or unable to pay for themselves. One language – on forms, in television and in public administration – is cheaper than two. Rural bus services and village schools incur higher per capita costs, and supporting these from public resources is a drain on the national economy. The intermediate institutions, then, cannot justify or defend themselves with reference to either of the poles of moral debate – that is, to the only courts of appeal that human rights discourse allows to exist.

Any moral discourse that is strung out between two polarities will therefore have the net effect, in the long run, of crushing the intermediate-sized institutions. That can even include the family, which is undoubtedly the biggest hindrance to the immediate gratification of personal wishes but can even fall foul of censures from the opposite end of the individual–all polarity. Think of Norman Tebbit's famous advice to the unemployed to 'get on their bikes' – extended families and adherence to place must yield to the demands of labour mobility in the interests of expanding the gross national product.

The argumentations of Left and Right, then, have tended to the same end: the breaking down of all durable institutions bigger than the individual and smaller than the state. Margaret Thatcher could rail against those who were resisting the selling off of council houses because, as she rightly pointed out, socialists needed a constituency of people who depended on the state. But – pots and kettles. Her own best intentions notwithstanding, right-wing policies tended (albeit via a different route) towards the same end: an atomized society with nothing intact between the worker and Whitehall, between the clerk and Capitol Hill.

Admittedly, this picture of economic liberals and social

collectivists on the Right versus economic collectivists and social libertarians on the Left has blurred considerably in recent years. The Right blinked first and, despite the Iron Lady's best intentions, the Thatcher and Reagan revolutions tended to spill over into generalized doctrines of libertarianism among some – though by no means all – of their supporters. In more recent years, it has been the Left that has shifted, since the results of state intervention began looking increasingly threadbare and then, with the collapse of communism in eastern Europe, socialism became a creed for cranks. First Bill Clinton stole the Republicans' clothes in the interests of getting elected. Then New Labour in Britain tried the same tack and were rewarded with finally breaking the Tory stranglehold on power in the elections of 1997. In Germany, the Social Democrat Gerhard Schröder ('Herr Blair') managed the same feat by openly pleading with the German electorate to emulate the new British model.

By the beginning of the twenty-first century, the triumph of the Left (or of those political forces that still liked to designate themselves as such) was the triumph of individualism and of the individualistic understanding of human rights. The left-wing values they had retained were those of sexual and social libertarianism. The values they had quietly ditched were those of economic collectivism (or socialism) in the interests of free markets – even if Tony Blair still liked to insist, to cover his embarrassment, that his was really a 'third way'.

It was John Stuart Mill (1806–73) who was the principal prophet of the onward march of individualistic rights. His *On Liberty* of 1859 was the classic tract of political and moral liberalism for several generations of university students and intellectuals. He pointed out the dangers that ensued, not only from a government issuing wrong laws rather than right ones, but from issuing 'any mandates at all in things with which it ought not to meddle'. He feared the 'tyranny of the majority' who 'may desire to oppress a part of their number'.[5] Twentieth-century confessionalist and ethnic nationalist regimes have confirmed how well founded such fears might be.

However, Mill extended his argumentation (about the need to limit the powers of even democratic governments) into the arena of social relations. He wanted protection 'against the tyranny of the prevailing opinion and feeling, against the tendency of society to impose, by other means than civil penalties, its own ideas and practices as rules of conduct on those who dissent from them'.[6] He did not, in any case, mean quite what he said. His libertarianism was a self-serving plea for protection against Victorian, evangelical-inspired sexual propriety – and Mill was living with another man's wife. On other issues, however, where Mill felt himself to be safely in the majority, he was not above reversing his own arguments. Thus he urged the eradication of the Irish language as a barrier to the economic and social advancement of the Irish people as a whole. This should give pause for thought to those who assume that 'Victorian hypocrisy' was a monopoly of the upholders of morality and never indulged in, as here, by 'brave' moral dissidents.

Even if we take Mill completely seriously, however, he was nevertheless asking for the moon. Unless the present reader is alone in the house while perusing this page (perhaps even enthroned somewhere in private – stranger things have been known), then he or she is doubtless disporting himself or herself in a manner that takes account of 'the prevailing opinion and feeling' of others. Everything that we do, from the broad features of our lives to the minutiae of dress, posture and gesture, falls within generally recognized parameters of acceptability. 'Liberty' from these constraints is an illusion, for we can hardly live without them. Nevertheless, the tradition of viewing the moral dissident, the outrageous dresser, or just the person who is uncouth on principle, as somehow braver, more 'true to

himself or herself' and more 'liberated from social condi-
tioning' can be traced to this line of reasoning. In it, rights
discourse fuses with romanticism to create the myth of the
sovereign, autonomous individual.

## A test case: abortion

The case made here against human rights and in favour of
traditional 'obligations' may seem to many to be somewhat
theoretical and rooted in historical analysis rather than the
supposedly solid ground of pragmatism. Rights and duties,
it might be argued, are simply corollaries of one another, so
it does not much matter which system we propound. One
may teach that 'you must not rob Mary as she walks down
the street' or that 'Mary has a right to walk down the street
without being robbed'. Whichever code is followed, the
same result: Mary may conduct her business in safety.

I should counter that this is by no means the end of the
story, for the two systems of moral catechizing produce very
different states of mind in those who imbibe them. But let us
meet this objection (that rights and duties are virtual equivalents) on its own terms by looking also at more immediate
results. As a test case, let us consider the debate about the
moral status of abortion.

Supporters of the permissibility of abortion deploy many
arguments, but central to them all is that of 'a woman's right
to choose what to do with her body'. Christians and other
moral conservatives who standardly oppose abortion
counter with their own slogan: 'the child's right to life'.
Whose right will win?

In the worlds of politics and moral debate around us, the
victor in this argument is pre-ordained. The women who
wish to 'choose' – to say nothing of the feckless boyfriends
and anxious parents who wish to urge them on, and the
much larger numbers of people with an interest in the avail-
ability of abortion to underwrite their 'sexual freedom' – are

with us, voting and articulating their opinions. The unborn children are unable to speak and are reliant only on those who care about them and are unencumbered by anticipating a need to dispose of the consequences of their own sexual indiscretions. Hedonism wins: the child dies.

Now let us re-cast this debate in the language of obligations and duties. Who, in this circumstance of an undesired pregnancy, has an obligation to whom? Again, the winner is pre-ordained. It is the child. For clearly the woman and her sexual partner – and perhaps others too – have a duty to nurture and protect it. To argue otherwise, it would be necessary to say that the child has a duty to die so that the mother and her partner (or relatives, or society) are not inconvenienced.

Now it is not completely ridiculous to insist that, in certain circumstances, a person does indeed have a duty to die. Such a duty is implied, for example, when a war criminal who pleads that he was 'only following orders' while under a threat to his own life is sentenced anyway. The person who finds himself in such an extreme situation has a duty to die rather than to participate in such foul actions as constitute a war crime.

But the situation of an (unknowingly) unwanted baby in the womb is not such a circumstance. In any case, the baby is unable to fulfil such an obligation in his or her own person – only to have it imposed from outside by the surgeon's knife. To speak of 'a duty to die' in such a case is presumably nonsensical.

If we frame the question in terms of human rights, abortion wins. If we ask instead about moral obligations, the child lives. In both cases, the 'answer' was already present in the question.

This issue also illustrates the repeated mistake made by Christians in lightly accepting the premises of their opponents, and then finding themselves powerless to resist the unwelcome conclusions. We wish to 'buy' the Western world-view while subtracting the elements that we do not like. But those elements are the fruit of the poisoned tree. And a bad tree, as someone once observed, will not yield good fruit. To resist the conclusions of our opponents, we should be well advised to reject their premises as well, or else we will lose every argument. Indeed, we are, observably, doing so.

## Three kinds of 'rights'

When discussing 'rights' language, we can discern three kinds of meaning. The first is that of empirical or legal rights, as described in an actual law code. This, of course, is reflected in Scripture, with abundant references to 'the rights of the poor' – that is, those guaranteed protections of the poor, orphans and widows given in the law of Israel.[7] Israel, of course, was a special case, in that its law emanated from God himself. 'Rights' terminology, however, could be – and was – used in reference to the provisions of other law codes which claimed no such origin.

The second possible meaning of 'rights' – and one also known to Scripture – is the inverse sense of an obligation earned, either by dint of a service performed or by being due to one's special position. So Paul asks rhetorically whether a potter has 'the right to make out of the same lump of clay some pottery for noble purposes and some for common use'.[8] To the Corinthians, he urges his own 'rights': to food and drink; to take a believing wife on his journeys for the gospel; to be paid for his Christian work. In fact, however, he repeatedly affirms that he has not used any of these rights.[9] But they exist by virtue of the obligations that his service has put upon those whom he has served, and perhaps also by his special place of leadership in – or at any rate of relationship to – the Christian churches. In the same way, we might say that our parents have a 'right' to our obedience when we are children and to our respect when we are grown up; it is a correlative to the duties of the young to obey and, later, at least to honour their fathers and mothers.

The third meaning is that of human rights itself: a moral right that is claimed simply by virtue of one's existence. This, we have observed, is a concept foreign to Scripture, and indeed to all of the world before the eighteenth century. It might be claimed that Job 36.6 is a biblical instance of 'human rights'. The NIV has: 'He [God] does not keep the wicked alive but gives the afflicted their rights.' 'Rights' here, it might be argued, cannot be empirical or legal rights, since the speaker is no earthly king, but God himself; it must therefore be abstract morality that is being discussed. We do not insist on the objection that the 'rights' might be enshrined in the Mosaic law, with God as its ultimate origin, for the NIV translation rests on a linguistic misunderstanding and consequent *eisegesis* (that is, a reading back into Scripture of ideas not derived from it). The AV, which has no intrinsic superiority to modern versions, has at least the merit of preceding the eighteenth-century concept of human rights. It translates the verse: 'He preserveth not the life of the wicked: but giveth right to the poor.' The singular 'right' is clearly a seventeenth-century synonym for 'justice', a reading confirmed by reference to the Hebrew *mishpat*, which means 'justice' or 'a favourable verdict'. Job 36.6, then, is no basis for 'rights' as a free-floating idea, not necessarily attached to a specific legal code.

Human rights are not the correlative of obligations, as its defenders might claim, but the converse; instead of being a mirror-image way of expressing duties, it is – in its cumulative effects, even if not explicitly – a denial of them. That is why all of the enculturation mechanisms of turn-of-the-millennium Western societies – education, the Babel of the media, peer pressure – have bred two generations with little or no sense of their own obligations. At most, conservative-minded politicians whine about the 'need to balance rights with obligations'. Such blandishments are good for raising a cheer, but they do so to no discernible social effect, for the 'obligations' that the audience have in mind are always those of others, never of themselves; their own enculturation processes are too strong to work in any way other than to highlight grievances – and so to see themselves as sinned against, not as sinning.

## Corporate guilt, personal sinlessness

The only obligations, in human-rights discourse, are corporate, not personal. If the poor are starving, we need a new law or a new tax, not more generous individuals – for charity would be patronizing, and thus an affront to the rights of the recipients, as well as implying personal obligations all round. If we feel guilty at all, it is the false guilt of belonging to an allegedly oppressive group – male, white, middle-class, able-bodied – rather than for anything we have actually done, or failed to do. In consequence we may feel guilty for what we are (that is, for something that cannot be rectified) but not for what we do (that is, for what we can repent of and amend). As members of a group or groups, we are full of ridiculous self-loathing; as individuals, however, we acknowledge no shortcomings (certainly no specific ones) at all. To do the latter would be to accept the burden of obligations, which would be to trammel our freedom, and so compromise our rights.

The person who is aware of his or her rights is liable to adopt an attitude of self-righteous indignation at precisely the point of being most selfish and most demanding. Human rights are certainly implicated in the culture of aggressive self-assertion by petty miscreants, especially among the young. 'Give it here!' 'How dare you expect something of me?' 'Don't I have a right to do as I want?' Such a person will view any residual obligations that might be urged upon him or her – that is, any last echoes of that earlier, all-but-extinguished moral universe – as an imposition. Indeed, such a person observably does so – in the street, in the classroom, in the domestic altercation. Almost certainly, he or she will reach for the epithet 'arbitrary' (or similar) to describe it. Equally certainly, he or she will call into question the moral authority of the person urging the call of duty. If, as with the duties of wayward parents to care for their child, the obligations are imposed, not by a person or persons, but by nature itself, such a person will plead his or her cause as a social unfortunate, to whom socialized help should be given – as a matter of right.

'Help should *be* given' – such a manner of speaking is hardly accidental. Moral discourse under the tutelage of human rights has seen the most abundant profusion of passive verbs since all schoolboys were required to learn second-form Latin. We wish, not for people to give to the poor, but for 'financial support to be supplied'; not for individuals to care but for 'care to be given'; not for people to provide for the needy, but for 'provision to be made'. Support without supporters, care without carers, provision without providers; to relapse into normal, active verbs would be to highlight the obvious: that moral action requires moral actors – and so to revert to personal obligations. To avoid this uncomfortable reality, public discourse through the Babel of the media adopts a curious duck-speak on moral questions, as if it is all a matter of better 'systems' and bureaucracy without any of us having to accept that we have duties. Only people such as we who have forgotten the real meaning of moral (or immoral) actions can speak of 'provision of care' (say for the sick or elderly), thereby depersonalizing the second most personal verb (after 'love', of course, which has already been hijacked by sex) in the language, in our desperate effort to bureaucratize it and so evade the force of personal obligations.

But people with no sense of obligations are people with no sense of personal sin. No wonder that Christians are quite unable to evangelize effectively in this environment – without, that is, resorting to shallow emotionalism or blandishments about the 'benefits' of 'coming to know Jesus'. If I have no obligations, then there are no duties that I have failed to fulfil, no forbidden acts that I should feel guilty about having done. I cannot envisage myself as a sinner, not even before a holy God. The central thrust of Christian evangelism is thereby rendered ridiculous.

Little wonder that the sense of personal sinfulness, even among Christians, is largely superficial. And that superficiality is reflected in our lives. We see ourselves overwhelmingly as sinned against, not as sinning; as standing in need of a little therapy, more self-esteem and some assertiveness training, not of forgiveness.

Who has the persuasive power to convict of sin such persons as we have become? Well did John record Jesus' saying that it must be the Holy Spirit who would 'convict the world of guilt in regard to sin and righteousness and judgment'![10] Never has it been further beyond the capacity of mere evangelists to do so. Human beings have been ducking responsibility since Eden; it is only our own generation that has had the ingenuity to reject it as a category! We have no need of a Saviour; in our own minds, at least, we are already perfect. The Babel tells us so.

# Killing the past: tradition, progress and un-progress

## The authority of tradition

In almost all traditional cultures, including our own before the modern period, wisdom and right behaviour consisted in following tradition and the ways of one's ancestors. On this view, the world is not our own, but a trust from our forebears to be handed on to our posterity in something like the shape in which it was handed down to us. Not that most people in traditional cultures thought globally, or even 'nationally' (where that is not an anachronistic term); the horizons of most people were fixed by the locality, the town or the village.

Reverence for the elderly was natural enough when most people died in their 40s and few survived into old age. Old people were indeed 'wise', for they alone had the experience to guide decision-making. They would remember the customary behaviour for encounters that were out of the ordinary. An old person might be the only source on hand to give a village population a clue as to how to deal with a famine or an imminent attack by enemies; old people would, at least, remember how it had been dealt with last time – and the fact of survival would mean that the opinion given would carry the weight of success.

Reverence for the old led naturally enough to reverence for ancestors. The ancestors were wise; they had known what to do. Their ways had the status of authority. Many historical sources show that periods of conscious cultural change, such as the Christianization of a tribe or kingdom (or, later, the Reformation), occasioned acute anxiety among ordinary people. In most human societies, the ways of the ancestors were to be revered and followed. 'We' have survived until now because our forebears acted as they did. Are we really wiser than they? Will we take the risk of breaking from the patterns of behaviour that have kept us alive? To make such a break, one would have to be very sure of oneself. But pre-moderns did not, by and large, have the benefit of assertiveness therapy and courses to help them boost their self-esteem; few were confident that they knew better than their peers and ancestors.

Many pre-moderns perceived that there were differences between the present in which they lived and the image of the past (as often as not, idealized), which it was their duty to reflect, and they therefore judged their own age as deficient on that count. Innovation and initiative were not prized qualities, but serious faults. What had precipitated the Fall of mankind, the expulsion from Eden and the abrupt end of the primeval Golden Age if not the actions of a pair who had taken the initiative? The Golden Age stood for an idealized past, which the present could never really live up to. Yet one must try; it was the common duty to hold on to received ways of doing things in order to prevent further slippage and decline. One has only to glance at political or religious discourse in the sixteenth and seventeenth centuries to see this mental process still at work.

## Strained appeals to 'the past' in a changing world

Where, however, thinkers were inclined to find the traditions and received patterns themselves to be defective, as the artists and writers of the Renaissance did, then they appealed over the head of the immediate, medieval sources of those traditions to the more distant – and so more authoritative – past of ancient Greece and Rome. Indeed, it is from the Renaissance (the 'rebirth' of classical learning) that we get our term 'Middle Ages': these were the despised *media eva*, which stood between two periods of culture and learning, namely the present and the true benchmark of the Greek and Roman ages. Similarly, the sixteenth-century reformers responded to the Roman Catholics' 'common sense' criticism that Protestantism was departing from tradition with the charge that it was the papacy that had departed from the tradition of the early Church. Once again, one could appeal over the head of the present and the immediate past to a more distant, more authoritative past.

Such convoluted arguments simultaneously demonstrated the strength of the authority of tradition and began to put it under strain. This is brought out even more clearly in the political arguments of the English Civil War period. Thus the regime of Charles I (English king 1625–49), was both defended by its (few) friends and denounced by its (more numerous) enemies as either keeping or failing to keep faith with the constitution of the past. When the Long Parliament debated, in 1641, whether to abolish bishops, whose controversial high churchmanship had been such an important plank of Charles's government, George Digby, the moderate royalist, pleaded, 'Let us not destroy bishops, but make them such as they were in primitive times.'

The royalist soldiers in the Civil War cried that they were 'For the King!' but their opponents claimed to be fighting 'For King and Parliament!' The latter could not bring themselves to admit that they were actually fighting against the King, even as they did so, for that would have been to admit that they did not have tradition on their side – and therefore that they were in the wrong. Socially necessary myths about 'rescuing the King from his advisers' were brought into play to suppress the reality that some people, at least, were beginning to oppose tradition and its attendant deference to received authority.

Later that decade, the parliamentarian Henry Ireton, Cromwell's son-in-law, defended himself against the Leveller radical Colonel Rainborough, who wished the vote to be given to all adult males, at the Putney Debates of 1647 thus: 'I am sure that if we look upon . . . what was originally the constitution of this kingdom . . . those that choose the representers [are] the persons in whom all land lies, and those in corporations in whom all trading lies.'[1] Even as he fought against the King, and even as he made a place in his ideal constitution for the new trading class ('those in corporations in whom all trading lies'), Ireton nevertheless claimed that his theories rested on 'what was originally the constitution of this kingdom'!

When it came to executing Charles in January 1649, all kinds of mental gymnastics had to be gone through to demonstrate that Charles had been a traitor to himself, a conception that most contemporaries found frankly incredible.

Meanwhile, the real radicals, such as Colonel Rainborough and the Levellers, had to invent a mythical past in order to claim tradition as in any sense belonging to themselves. According to the theory of the 'Norman yoke', England before the conquest of 1066 had consisted of happy, self-governing peasants; it was only the intrusion of William the Conqueror that had made English kingship into a system of political subjection. Thus they, the Levellers, were the true upholders of the authority of the past.[2]

It is the very absurdity of this last argument that illustrates the strength of the idea that underlies it; so powerful was the 'common sense' that tradition was authoritative, that potential innovators were forced to desperate lengths to prove that they were somehow, appearances notwithstanding, faithful to the ways of their forebears. In the common parlance of the day, the term 'innovation' was uniformly a term of abuse; one hastened to fasten the label around the neck of one's opponents and to disentangle it by any means or argument possible from around one's own. To make the charge of 'innovation' stick was to demonstrate, *ipso facto*, that the other fellow was in the wrong. In this, seventeenth-century Englishmen were at one with all the world before the Enlightenment and with much of the (non-Western) world after it.

But the acceleration of change that would culminate in the Industrial Revolution was already under way, which explains why so many of their arguments predicated on 'tradition' and opposition to 'innovation' were so odd. They themselves were changing but could not bring themselves to admit it. A society that genuinely and consistently damned 'innovation' and personal initiative would fare poorly in economic terms – as the Middle Ages had done, and as some Third World countries still do. But seventeenth-century England was in the throes of becoming a commercial economy, dominated by those very people 'in corporations in whom all trading lies' for whom Ireton would have secured the vote, even as he wanted to keep ordinary people from sharing that privilege on the grounds of tradition.

Ireton had been well to the left of centre by the standards of his day. By the late eighteenth century, however, the parliamentarian Edmund Burke counted as a conservative for defending the same position. According to him, the 'Glorious Revolution' of 1688–89 (when James II had been ejected and replaced by his daughter Mary and her husband William of Orange) and all of the other constitutional and religious shifts in English history had really been aimed at maintaining the status quo; that was the reason why they had been legitimate:

> We wished at the period of the Revolution [the 'Glorious Revolution' of 1688/9], and do now wish, to derive all we possess as *an inheritance from our forefathers* . . . .
> All the reformations we have hitherto made, have proceeded upon the principle of reference to antiquity . . .

He looked aghast on the French Revolution of his own day, which did not meet this criterion, but espoused instead the principles of democracy, egalitarianism and progress: 'The very idea of the fabrication of a new government, is enough to fill us with disgust and horror.'[3]

As we have seen, the concept of the wrongness of innovation had been coming under increasing strain in Western countries for a couple of centuries before Burke. As a result, the claims of many factions (or of Burke in this example) to be 'really' upholding tradition became more fanciful, complicated and far-fetched. And this growing difficulty was due to the quickening pace of change in Western life, economy and society. It was becoming harder and harder to square reality, or to justify one's own aspirations, with the ideal picture of following tradition.

### Breaking the shackles of tradition: 'progress' as common sense

Indeed, even as Burke wrote, this picture was falling apart. The ideal of adherence to tradition was being discarded as part and parcel of that whole series of wider intellectual changes that we call the Enlightenment. In part, it was a coming to terms with the fact of change – change understood, not as a lamentable necessity imposed from outside or by internal decline, but as a positive development brought about by a society seeking to control its own destiny and to free itself from the limitations of the past.

Tom Paine's famous work *The Rights of Man* was penned specifically as a rejoinder (and a vitriolic one at that) to

Burke's attack on the French Revolution and its principles. The authority of tradition could never limit what ought or ought not to be done:

> The vanity and presumption of governing beyond the grave, is the most ridiculous and insolent of all tyrannies. Man has no property in man; neither has any generation a property in the generations which are to follow. . . Every generation is, and must be, competent to all the purposes which its occasions require. It is the living, and not the dead, that are to be accommodated . . . Mr Burke is contending for the authority of the dead over the rights and freedom of the living.[4]

Paine's ideal polity was America, of whose revolution against British rule in the 1770s he had been a principal instigator. America was the place in which the authority of tradition could be overthrown; it was a new world, geographically removed from the old one and so susceptible of fresh beginnings. Its (white European) populace was constituted, to no small degree, of those who had rejected the orthodoxies of the Old World and had fled there for refuge:

> So effectually had the tyranny and the antiquity of habit established itself over the mind, that no beginning could be made in Asia, Africa, or Europe, to reform the political condition of man. . . From the rapid progress which America makes in every species of improvement, it is rational to conclude, that if the governments of Asia, Africa, and Europe, had begun on a principle similar to that of America . . . that those countries must, by this time, have been in a far superior condition to what they are. Age after age has passed away, for no other purpose than to behold their wretchedness.[5]

The ideal of 'progress' was born, along with its counterpart, the rejection of tradition. History was destined to move onwards and upwards. The religious wars of the sixteenth and seventeenth centuries had been left behind and *raison d'état* had taken over, not only in the counsels of European governments (where, in truth, it had never been absent), but also as a public ideal. Scientific and technological break-throughs were accelerating on all fronts; the wisdom of the past now loomed less large than did the newly accumulating mountains of knowledge. Economic progress was palpable, and the Industrial Revolution was creating a benign circle of self-sustaining economic growth. Perhaps best of all, the European powers were entering on a period of global dom-ination that would continue until after the First World War. That domination would be political, administrative, mili-tary and economic; taken together, it was proof irrefutable of the superiority of Western culture and values, which had produced the instruments of this domination: better navigation and communications, finer steel and superior weaponry.

Once this shift in outlook had occurred (or rather, had begun to occur, for it progressed at different speeds in dif-ferent Western countries and in different social segments of those countries), unfolding events tended to confirm its rightness. Living standards were rising during the nine-teenth and early twentieth centuries. Industrial output was increasing. Western power was growing.

This confidence (complacency, some might say) was well expressed by the historian Edward Gibbon (1737–94), who argued for 'the pleasing conclusion that every age of the world has increased, and still increases, the real wealth, the happiness, the knowledge, and perhaps the virtue of the human race'. Lest this should be thought surprising in one whose subject was, after all, the overthrow of Roman civilization by the barbarians, he nevertheless insisted, in the face of his own evidence, that 'Barbarians . . . before they can conquer must cease to be barbarous'. The 'system of arts and laws and manners, which so advantageously distinguish, above the rest of mankind, the Europeans and their colonies', therefore, made them invulnerable to overthrow. This was because any other culture would have to adopt European mores before it could progress 'in the science of war', a process that, 'as we may learn from the example of Russia', would also produce 'a proportionable improvement in the arts of peace and civil policy' of a kind that would cease to make such peoples dangerous.[6] That his choice of example was less than entirely felicitous it was left to the twentieth century to demonstrate.

Saint-Simon (1760–1825), the French social theorist who, as a young man, had joined in the American struggle for independence, wrote in 1814 that 'the Golden Age of mankind does not lie behind us, but before; it lies in the perfection of the social order. Our forefathers did not see it; one day our children will reach it. It is for us to clear the way.'[7] Previous generations had generally believed that the 'Golden Age' did indeed lie behind us; that had been a part, at least, of the meaning of the Garden of Eden. In premodern societies, it had been the reason that tradition was to be followed. It was why, in some cultures, ancestors were to be venerated.

No longer. Darwin's evolutionism, after 1859, propagated the idea that our ancestors were apes. Before that, they had belonged to even more basic species. Progress, not retrogression, was the law of the universe. It was, as Herbert Spencer put it, 'not an accident, but a necessity . . . What we call evil and immorality must disappear. It is certain that man must become perfect.'[8]

Whether or not one subscribed to such fantasies, evil and immorality were now definitely associated, not with the perils of future change, but with the past – a past from which the present was liberating itself. Instead of being revered, the past was excoriated. The Marquis de Condorcet had been a leader in this field when he denounced the Middle Ages, whose

> only achievements were theological day-dreaming and superstitious imposture, [their] only morality religious intolerance. In blood and tears, crushed between priestly tyranny and military despotism, Europe awaited the moment when a new enlightenment would allow her to be reborn free, heiress to humanity and virtue.[9]

Condorcet, however, died in prison in 1793, a captive at the hands of the revolutionaries fighting for *'liberté, egalité, fraternité'*. Charles Dickens, in the next century, kept his study walls lined with dummy books, labelled *The Wisdom of our Ancestors*, with individual titles that read 'Ignorance', 'Superstition', 'The Block', 'The Stake', 'The Rack', 'Dirt' and 'Disease'. The smugness of this posture has been impossible to maintain in our own age; the twentieth century has been the bloodiest and, in the chimerical nature of its fascist and socialist utopianisms, the most superstitious of all. But the hatred of tradition – real tradition, as opposed to its sentimentalized, fancy-dress, museum-entombed version – has endured.

Ideas of progress carried profoundly negative implications, of course, not just for the Garden of Eden, but for religious ideas and churchly authority generally. Christian belief located authority in a past tradition and in an ancient text speaking of historical events. Religious spokesmen divided, as so often, more or less evenly between those who decried the new trends and those who were prepared to set the latest songs to a religious tune.

In the former camp was Pope Pius IX who, before having himself declared infallible by the First Vatican Council of 1869–70, issued the famous Syllabus of Errors of 1864, which condemned not only religious toleration, but also the idea that there could be any 'compromise with progress, liberalism and modern civilization'. The modernists of the French Revolution in 1789 had been anti-clerical, and indeed anti-Christian; Pius IX's pronouncements three-quarters of a century later reinforced a pattern of events whereby modernizing Westerners saw religion in general, and Roman Catholicism in particular, as obstructionist and obscurantist, dangerous if powerful and simply irrelevant otherwise. Nothing better sums up the continuing attitude of most Westerners towards religion in general, even if the focus has shifted recently towards what most people mindlessly refer to as 'fundamentalism' (by which they mean, of course, religious believers who fundamentally believe in their religion as an alternative world-view to Western secularity, rather than as a gloss of religious verbiage baptizing that secularity).

The Roman Catholic hierarchy's voice was not the only religious voice opposing the idea of 'progress', but it was certainly the shrillest. Abraham Kuyper left the Reformed ministry to establish and lead the Anti-Revolutionary Party in the Netherlands from 1879. This took its name from its opposition, 90 years after the event, to the principles of the French Revolution and a Calvinistic insistence that 'the *perspectives du paradis* cannot be realized on earth'.[10] Kuyper, like many conservative Protestants, remained uneasy, to say the least, about Darwin's theories.

Many others, however, were in the opposite camp, that of those who found it easy to legitimize the new emphasis on 'progress'. It was Protestantism, after all, that had encouraged the famous 'work ethic' and a whole host of other developments, from attitudes of mind to measurable shifts in social organization, that had made possible the meteoric industrial growth and the technical developments that supported it.

From the eighteenth century, more and more divines started to reject what, in 1743, William Worthington, Canon of York, called 'the Prejudice which Men in all Ages have against their own Times, and the vulgar Opinion, that the World grows worse and worse, Mankind more degenerate, and the Seasons more unfavourable'.[11] Jonathan Edwards, the great American revivalist and theologian, reflected the growing trend towards post-millennialism, the opinion that Christ would return, not in order to inaugurate a new Golden Age, but after it had already been ushered in on earth by human beings in the glowing future that lay ahead.

> Doubtless one nation shall be enlightened and converted, and one false religion and false way of worship exploded, after another . . . Satan's visible kingdom on earth shall be destroyed. His dominion has been much brought down already by the vial poured out on his throne in the Reformation; but then it shall be utterly destroyed. This [the coming triumph of the gospel] is most properly the time of the kingdom of heaven upon earth . . . It will be a time of great light and knowledge . . . Great knowledge shall prevail everywhere. It may be hoped, that then many of the Negroes and Indians may be divines, and that excellent books will be published in Africa, in Ethiopia, in Tartary, and other now the most barbarous countries . . . That will be a time of the greatest temporal [meaning, in this context, 'material'] prosperity.[12]

It all sounded wonderful. It also sounded remarkably like the events that were actually and visibly unfolding at the time: the conquest of heathen nations by Christian ones; shifts in the balance of power within Christendom, of a kind that Jonathan Edwards would have approved, beginning with the Reformation; the advance of knowledge of all kinds and the improvement of non-European peoples by their colonial masters; increasing prosperity. Such a transposition of the ideal of progress into a religious key was the common tune of Protestants for much of the eighteenth and nineteenth centuries, and even (in a greatly secularized form) among liberal Protestants during the first part of the twentieth. By then, however, it had become a parody of Edwards's vision, ready prey for C. S. Lewis's mockery, through the character of Reverend Straik, in his novel *That Hideous Strength*.

What scientists were saying in respect of evolution, and clergymen by a drastic reshuffling of the apocalyptic schedule, historians were echoing in respect of their theories about the direction of human affairs. The Whig theory of history held sway (though not, before the 1930s, under that name) in British academia until the Second World War, and in some schoolrooms for a while longer. Its chief tendency was to trace the rise of modernity, and in particular those aspects of it that appealed to nineteenth-century liberals: the growing power of parliaments and the declining power of monarchs; the move towards democracy; the emergence of religious toleration; commercial development; the rise of universal literacy and education. As Lord Macaulay (1800–59) put it in his *History of England*, it was his intention to relate

> how . . . the authority of law and the security of property were found to be compatible with a liberty of discussion and of individual action never before known; how, from the auspicious union of order and freedom, sprang a prosperity of which the annals of human affairs had furnished no example; how our country, from a state of ignominious vassalage, rapidly rose to the place of umpire among European powers; how her opulence and her martial glory grew together, . . . how a gigantic commerce gave birth to a maritime power, compared with which every other maritime power, ancient or modern, sinks into insignificance, . . . how in Asia, British adventurers founded an empire not less splendid and more durable than that of Alexander.[13]

As with Edwards, it was really all very satisfactory.

Later historians who would, from the 1930s, be labelled 'Whig' differed in subtlety but not in substance. History was moving onwards and upwards. Even the Marxist ideology, which supplanted such readings of history in Western universities from the mid-twentieth century, retained a core belief in progress: the Marxists knew where history was going and that the destination was a better place than the present – though even the present was better than the past. As John Gray tellingly puts it, 'Marx's absurd idea of "the end of history", in which communism triumphs and destructive conflict then vanishes from the world, is transparently a secular mutation of Christian apocalyptic beliefs'.[14] More precisely, he might have added, it is a mutation of postmillennialism.

Marxist execrations of capitalism have often drowned out, to the untrained ears of non-Marxists, the rueful, ironic appreciation of capitalism and all of the other elements that the Whig historians so much admired. Capitalism was a transitional stage of economy and society, on the way to the socialist utopia that the Soviet Union and its satellites supposedly embodied. Traditional societies needed to go through a bourgeois industrial phase in order to bring into being the 'proletariat', or industrial working class, that would create the communist revolution. This is the central point of the opening chapter of Marx's and Engels's *Communist Manifesto*.

From that standpoint, unfortunately, neither Russia in 1917 nor, still less, China in 1948 was 'ready' for a proletarian dictatorship, having hardly any actual proletariat to speak of. Marxists had to go through all manner of *post facto* rationalizations and other contortions: the rise of 'Marxism–Leninism' and 'Marxism–Leninism–Maoism' (that is, Marxism versions 2 and 3) was necessary to 'explain' the departure of actuality from the previous theories.

Nonsense or not, the influential nature of Marxist and quasi-Marxist ideas in the West is a prominent example of the generalized belief in progress and emancipation from the past. Indeed, the very label 'progressive', which still lingers on as an approving epithet for left-wing causes (along with its negative corollary, 'reactionary', for right-wing ideas), remains as a linguistic fossil of the now defunct notion that a speaker knows where history is going. More realistically, it is a mere signal that the user concurs in the (by now traditional) rejection of tradition.

Much in the preceding paragraphs has, alas, lapsed into intellectual history, as we have been citing the words of the great and the influential. But the ideas that they expressed (or formulated, in some cases) were of considerable gravity, at least as measured by the speed with which they sank down through the social strata to permeate the language and thought forms of common parlance. To an extent, this has already been indicated by some of our examples. The philosophers of the Enlightenment may have been addressing an élite audience, but Macaulay in the nineteenth century was speaking to the great middle class of England. His contemporary, Dickens, was accessible to all who were merely literate and even, via the practice of reading aloud, to children and adults who were not. Jonathan Edwards may have been one of the greatest of America's intellectuals, but his ideas on this subject (which were not, in any case, original to him) were reflected in the preachments of thousands of pulpits – whether the subject in hand was social affairs or salvation, history or hell-fire – until they became part of what ordinary people considered to be common sense. The world was getting better and could be expected to continue to do so; that's all there was to it.

## Progress as passé

The current generation of Westerners does not share this sense any longer. Progress ceased to be common sense sometime between the First World War and the 1960s.

The two world wars destroyed this easy assurance for many, and at least punctured it for the rest. The threat of nuclear annihilation hovered like a dark cloud even over the sky-rocketing Western living standards of the decades after 1945. The dawning realization, from the early 1970s onwards, that infinite economic and population growth into finite global resources was a nonsense made any talk of inevitable progress seem silly. The rise of pop-existentialism among the young and the loss of confidence in what we have recently learned to call 'metanarratives' reinforced the demise of the 'progress' myth – even if political lefties continued to use epithets such as 'progressive' and 'reactionary' to give the impression that they knew what they were talking about.

A similar relic of a now generally exploded way of thinking is the use of the mindless phrase 'in this day and age'. ('Fancy finding that in this day and age!'; 'How can this be tolerated in this day and age?' and so on.) In essence, it expresses several assumptions at once:

(a) that I know where history is going;
(b) that this destination is better than the past;
(c) that certain practices and beliefs are foredoomed to extinction
(d) . . . and I know which ones; and
(e) that outrage and disgust are justifiable responses when confronted with clear evidence that I'm wrong.

Of course, scientists and technologists continue to stand on the shoulders of their predecessors. They take progress-to-date as their starting point, and build on that. In that sense, scientific and technological progress continues. Despite wavering public confidence in 'science' and 'scientists', most people expect progress of this sort to continue, along with the economic benefits that might be hoped to accrue from it.

Beyond this, however, progress as a general descriptor of human expectations about the future is dead. What remains is an ingrained alienation from tradition and the authority of the past. One can be sentimental about 'the good old days', but most Westerners are certain that, not only is the past a foreign country, but its ideas were bad ideas, its morals bad morals (or, at any rate, too demanding), its social structures oppressive and its theories about the world and its religious beliefs unworthy of our serious attention. Beyond a series of object lessons – or as ammunition in some present ideological conflict – it has nothing to teach us. C. S. Lewis saw this state of mind looming even in the 1940s. For people such as himself, who had been steeped and saturated in the literature of antiquity, 'the Present has always appeared as one section in a huge continuous process' of past and future. For his contemporaries, however,

> the Present occupies almost the whole field of vision. Beyond it, isolated from it, and quite unimportant, is something called 'The Old Days' – a small, comic jungle in which highway men, Queen Elizabeth, knights-in-armour, etc., wander about.[15]

The populations of traditional societies may have had no clearer a grasp of the actual events of their own histories than does ours; as often as not those events were conflated or otherwise transmogrified into timeless myths. But the present did not occupy the whole field of their vision, nor was the past a 'comic jungle'. That Westerners, by contrast, have so successfully liberated themselves from their own past is no small part of their own sense of rootlessness. (Think of the famous complaint of Generation X: 'We have no identity.') From the standpoint of non-Westerners, it is a measure of barbarism. The world of yesterday has no relevance for us, for today we can invent it afresh. What else, after all, does the very idea of 'America' mean?

# Impersonal states

*How to be an Alien* was a comic masterpiece and sold briskly in the decades after the Second World War. First printed in 1946, it was in its 24th edition by 1971 when I discovered it as a teenager. The author, George Mikes, was a Hungarian Jew who had come to the UK for a fortnight in 1938 and, very wisely in the light of the political situation, had never gone back. His little book was a send-up of the British and of Britishness. Most of the characteristics of his new compatriots that he chose to delineate have since disappeared (except among the elderly) or, in one or two cases, have become more widely shared – and so no longer distinctively Anglo-Saxon. In the latter category is that of public service. His chapter 'Civil Servant' begins:

> There is a world of difference between the English Civil Servant and the continental. On the Continent (not speaking now of the Scandinavian countries), Civil Servants assume a certain military air. They consider themselves little generals . . . they cannot withdraw armies so they withdraw permissions . . . they cannot lose battles so they lose documents instead. They consider that the sole aim of human society is to give jobs to Civil Servants. A few wicked individuals, however (contemptible little groups of people who are not Civil

Servants), conspire against them, come to them with various requests, complaints, problems, etc., with the sole purpose of making a nuisance of themselves. These people get the reception they deserve.

Having sketched the body of 'continental' civil servants, Mikes then contrasts them with their British counterparts and tellingly concludes:

On the Continent rich and influential people, or those who have friends, cousins, brothers-in-law, tenants, business associates, etc., in an office may have their requests fulfilled. In England there is no such corruption and your obedient servant just will not do a thing whoever you may be. And this is the real beauty of democracy.[1]

The humour, of course, rests on a caricature of reality – or at least on a caricature of general perceptions. And the common perception was that, whereas 'continental' civil servants used their positions as a vehicle for personal advancement and for furthering the interests of their friends and relatives, their incorruptible British (or 'English') equivalents did no such thing. His punch line was that both were alike susceptible to the indolence and lack of urgency that characterize bureaucracy and the public sector everywhere. So in Britain, 'your obedient servant . . . will not do a thing whoever you may be'. No doubt the 'servant' was fortified by the aggressive egalitarianism that characterized the immediate post-war generation of demobilized British ex-servicemen, an egalitarianism that prompted countless petty confrontations during the 1940s, 1950s and 1960s: the spoken or implied 'Don't you know who I am?' was met with 'I don't care who you are, mate' (or by the policeman's 'Hey, Sarge, there's a bloke here wot doesn't know who he is!'). By the 1970s at the latest, the well-connected had given up even trying to pull rank.

If the ideal of 'disinterested public service' has since come to characterize most of western Europe (though the old habits linger on in corners), the process of change has barely started in much of the non-West. When a friend of mine delivered a new four-wheel-drive vehicle to a church in sub-Saharan Africa recently, he took plenty of luggage. He is an elder of the congregation in Swansea, Wales, to which I once belonged and, on this journey, he had a supply of Bibles and literature for the people he was to visit, as well as a rich fund of other little necessaries and presents for various individual people. All of this was duly noted by the Zambian officials at a border post as they inspected the car and its contents. 'Well,' asked one of these officials, 'what have you brought for me?' My friend reached into his store and handed the fellow some tapes of Christian music. To his relief, the guard was delighted with this gift, and a few minutes later his vehicle was waved through.

Was the guard a Christian, that he was so easily satisfied with the prospect of listening to recorded worship? Or was he indifferent to the content of the music? Was he planning simply to turn his new acquisition into cash at the next opportunity? Statistically, the first possibility is by no means to be discounted simply because he was, by current Western standards, corrupt.

An acquaintance in Serbia takes a gift to the dentist as a matter of course on each visit. Some students do the same to their professors when they are about to take an exam. When a good friend of mine in Croatia withdrew from a degree programme, it was because she was unwilling to pay professors every time she took an exam – and one of them simply refused to pass any student who did not give him money. As she explained to me, Western friends find her story incredible; they cannot believe that, if this incident were reported to 'the authorities', nothing would be done. But nothing is done, and other Croatian friends confirm the frequency of the kind of experience she describes.

The world over, outside of the sheltered confines of a few Western countries, it is expected, as a matter of course, that policemen will use their authority to extract payment from members of the public. Motorists are a particularly easy target; who is to say or to prove whether you were, or were not, breaking the speed limit? And in cars more than a year or two old, there are any number of minute defects that might be held to constitute a chargeable infringement; if you do not give the policeman money, he will keep you by the roadside for as long as it takes to find such a defect. For he represents authority – and he has a gun. The fact that the amount payable to him is so often open to negotiation is illustrative of the real nature of the transaction taking place.

Some Swiss friends of mine experienced exactly this in Burkina Faso while this book was being written. They were stopped by a policeman who imposed a horrendously high fine, supposedly for being 'a hindrance to other traffic'. (The file of vehicles in front of them and behind them was all moving at walking pace!) My friends protested, whereupon the policeman obligingly cut the 'charge' by 50 per cent. The argument continued, and the fine was finally commuted to buying the policeman a grape juice. Few policemen are so reasonable. Police depredations of a more severe kind are evidenced *in extremis* in Albania, where a driver can expect to be stopped every few kilometres in order to be relieved of cash. But Albania is one of the most pre-modern of societies; milder forms of the same phenomenon are observable across most of the globe.

In the contemporary Western view, of course, all of these practices constitute corruption. Some of them would be deemed corrupt from other standpoints also, but the issues are not necessarily always clear-cut. It is only in recent times, and in a few Western countries, that strict definitions of 'corruption' have obtained. Even within living memory and even in the UK, 'the old school tie' – or membership of the Masons, or of the 'right' political party in local government dealings, or of a particular club, church or other affiliation – could bring significant advantages in getting a job, or winning a contract, or cutting a deal in court.

But the scope for such favouritisms has diminished drastically in recent years, and is narrowing all the time. All processes now have to be 'transparent' in Western countries – which is to say that the procedures of corporate bodies have to satisfy the hyper-egalitarian demands made of them by the new élite [*sic*], forcing them to be more and more circuitous in reaching their real objectives. 'Equal opportunities' have been taken to the point where even religious organizations have to justify themselves in each case if they wish to specify that their employees be co-religionists. Colleges and universities are now castigated as anti-egalitarian conspiracies and deprived of funds by government if they dare to select students on mere intelligence and achievement.

The distinction between 'private' and 'public' is very marked in the modern and post-modern West but was almost invisible in pre-modern societies and, accordingly, is not always well attended to in the non-West today. Indeed, it is no small part of the mutual difficulty that Westerners and non-Westerners have in understanding one another. The former consider the latter to be corrupt. The latter feel themselves harshly judged by criteria that are alien to their thought patterns and social experience and that threaten to depersonalize their societies in exactly the way that these principles have atomized Western social existence. It is yet another reason that the West is resented as a cultural bully.

Here, we are concerned with the implications that this private–public distinction has for political life and structures of authority. In these terms it is, in practice, the same as the distinction between personal and impersonal authority. By 'impersonal authority', of course, is meant 'the rule of law'; that is, the state of affairs whereby decisions large and small are made on the basis of agreed principles, laws, procedures and abstract ideas that have – or at least claim to have – general support, rather than being guided by the interests of the individual people who happen, for the moment, to occupy the relevant official positions. To modern Westerners, all of this is so 'obvious' that it requires a real effort of mind to stop and recognize just what it is that we take for granted when a Prime Minister or President leaves office after losing an election, or when police officers are forced to defend themselves and their actions in court, or when officials need to justify their actions before complaints commissions and the press.

We might all agree that 'impersonal authority' and 'the rule of law' are among the best cultural distinctives of the modern West, both in terms of a more just social order and (if not taken too far) in enhancing efficiency. More than almost any other Western characteristic, it is this that might help non-Westerners towards a better life. But then we need to recognize also that these attributes go against the grain, to some extent, of human behaviour. Neither are they easily attained by non-prosperous societies, where the pressure of, and people's unavoidable dependency on, immediate personal relationships for survival mean that 'impartiality' and 'disinterested public service' are luxuries that few can afford. Even in our own context, we can see that these ideas can be pushed to the point where they lose their original purpose. For even the impartial modernist bureaucrat is, in one unavoidable sense, realizing personal goals through his or her work: career ambitions, the satisfaction of a job well done, the rewards of altruism. If, in the interests of supposed 'monitoring' and 'accountability', we harass the teacher with ridiculous levels of paperwork, terrify the policeman with threats of complaints procedures at every turn, push the doctors and nurses into 'defensive medicine' in order to ward off law suits, then we will all be less well off, not better off. And serve us right.

## Personal and impersonal rule

Classical Greece and Rome apart, the concepts of the 'impersonal state' and of impersonal authority had their genesis in the early modern period. We can see this by juxtaposing the central assumptions of its two classic political texts. The first of these, Machiavelli's *The Prince*, was written at the start of the sixteenth century and exhibits premodern assumptions: it is a guide to a man, telling him how to rule. The second, written in the mid-seventeenth century, is Hobbes's *Leviathan*, which propounded a theory of 'the State', which (regardless of who or what is its ruler) must fulfil the first requirement of any conceivable civil society: the maintenance of order. The first book is about persons; the second concerns abstractions.

Hobbes, of course, was writing during the period of the English Civil War, a crisis that forced a number of radical thinkers to locate authority in ideas rather than in persons. Thus it was that Oliver Cromwell, a cavalry commander on the parliamentarian side in the 1640s, defended himself from accusations that his policy of promoting soldiers on merit – including non-gentlemen and religious sectarians – was wicked and subversive with the following: 'Sir, the state in choosing men to serve it, takes no notice of their opinions; if they be willing to serve it faithfully, that suffices.' Such abstractions were something new. Until that time, one man had agreed to serve another; now, men agreed to serve an intangible object.

In the three and a half centuries since Cromwell, the abstractions have won hands down in the West. There is now a sharp division between public and private spheres. Accordingly, the modern conception of the state may be called 'impersonal'; it has an existence regardless of who may be leading its government at a given moment. (I am here using 'personal' and 'impersonal' in a different – indeed in an opposite – sense to that employed by Roger Scruton in his recent book *The West and the Rest*. Scruton speaks of modern Western states as 'personal' in the sense that they are understood to have a 'corporate personality', that is, in the legal sense, just like a limited company or a public corporation. I do not differ from his analysis in the least – but I do think that emphasizing the legal aspect of 'personality' makes language less, rather than more, clear.)

The UK and the USA will continue to exist even if (which heaven forfend) the Prime Minister and the President were suddenly to perish or be incapacitated. In the mean time, neither of them is under any illusion that the loyalties and obedience that they command derive in any sense from their persons; rather, they are due entirely to the offices that they happen – at least until the next elections – to occupy. Our sense of belonging to the 'imagined community' of the 'state' is now so strong that we would obey monkeys just as well, if they occupied the same positions. Indeed, those who think them monkeys already do so.

Pre-modern models of authority, on the other hand, were – and are – personal in nature at every level, not just at the apex of power. England, for example, functioned in the sixteenth and seventeenth centuries on the patronage system: public office was used, quite deliberately and self-consciously, as a means for promoting the personal ends and influence of the one holding office. In order to get things done one had to cultivate the friendship and patronage of those in a position to help, and build a base of loyal and grateful clients who could bolster one's own position from below. Conrad Russell, one of the most respected – and certainly one of the wittiest – historians of the period, observes that 'It was normal to offer presents to officials, not necessarily as a bribe, but as part of a general relationship of goodwill between them and their clients.' He notes that the Chancellor of the Exchequer was paid an annual salary of just £26 13s. 4d. in the sixteenth century, and the Secretary of State a mere £100. Even at Tudor prices, this was a pitiful remittance for such senior positions. The positions were taken, not for the salary, but for a mixture of prestige, influence and the perquisites ('perks') of office:

> Most office-holders were paid fees by the public, at the rate of, say, 2s. 6d. for sealing an official document, or perhaps 1d. a line for writing it (this is one reason why official documents grew so long) . . . One of the most valuable perquisites of office was the right to appoint to some of the junior posts.[2]

Unsurprisingly, then, offices were filled with the friends, relatives and dependants of those with appointive power. The historian Derek Hirst agrees: 'If young men wanted university fellowships or if towns wanted changes to their charters, they had in a pre-professionalized age to find those who could help them to what they wanted.' This did not mean that merit played no part at all in such matters; since clients' performance reflected on their patrons, the latter were seldom keen to appoint idiots.[3]

In the absence (or rather, the weakness) of rules, regulations and abstract, impersonal systems, the authority wielded by officials in the pre-modern world was essentially personal. Nineteenth-century Russia provides an extreme example of this form of consciousness, but in diluted forms it was – and is – present elsewhere.

> Without a fresh ordinance, no [peasant] will carry out [a previous directive]: everyone thinks that this directive had been given 'for that time only' . . . It is time to pay taxes. One might expect everyone to know from experience that they must be paid when due, that they will not be omitted. And still, without a special and, moreover, stern directive no one . . . will pay. Perhaps [it is thought] they will manage without taxes. . . .

The historian Richard Pipes describes this attitude toward law as 'directives issued for no discernible reason and, therefore, binding only in so far as they are imposed by force'. An attorney who worked closely with a variety of *volost'* (the smallest rural administrative unit) courts recorded that

> I was never able to detect the existence of some kind of general formula which even the given *volost'* court would apply to concrete, frequently recurring questions. Everything was based on arbitrariness, and, moreover, not the arbitrariness of the court's members, consisting of peasants, but that of the *volost'* clerk, who awarded verdicts at his whim . . . The verdict of a *volost'* court was invariably seen as the result of pressures from one of the parties or of hospitality in the form of a bottle or two of vodka . . . Our one hundred million peasants lived, in their everyday life, without law.[4]

Pre-revolutionary Russia was an extreme example of pre-modern, even pre-civilized, values into the modern era. Nevertheless, several features of this mind-set persist. First and most importantly, the uncertainty of the state of the law in many (indeed, most) non-Western countries delivers actual jurisdiction into the hands of the office-holder at the grass roots of implementation. To that extent, authority remains 'personal', inhering in the one holding office rather than in some set of abstractions that it is merely his or her task to enact. In the second place, ordinary people assume decisions to be the result of insider dealings. Hence conspiracy theories are a standard mode of discourse about politics, whether international, national, local or merely petty and institutional. Conspiracy rhetoric is the classic language of the disempowered – though it is also a declaration exculpating oneself from responsibility even where one is not totally disempowered. It is more consoling to believe that bad things have happened as the result of a plot by 'them', rather than as action – or inaction – by 'us'.

Modern Westerners, by contrast, now expect all authority exercised at lower levels to be as impersonal as a state presidency. The office-holder is fulfilling a public function, nothing more. They take their salary at the end of the month and go home, like everybody else, to spend it in the private sphere of their lives. The thought that the judge, the policeman, the schoolteacher or the civil servant may prefer one person, or group of people, over another for any private motive of his or her own is now anathema.

Pre-modern states, however, could not – and cannot – afford to recompense their rulers and servants in ways that could ever compensate them for such lofty impartiality. Instead, they were 'personal' in the sense that they were governed by a ruler who commanded the personal loyalty of his (or occasionally, her) subjects. The same thing applied at lower levels of authority. In those circumstances, the idea that a person holding a position of authority is somehow acting improperly by using it for personal gain seems ridiculous. Of course such positions will be so used; that is part of the meaning of the authority. (Obviously, if an official could be shown to have robbed their master, the king, then that would be a much more serious matter.)

In the Middle Ages, all authority had been personal, and as the medieval situation slowly gave way to the rise of modern bureaucracies and office-holding, so the positions created were used – as with George Mikes's 'continental' civil servants – for the exercise of personal influence. It was not resented by those who did not hold office; rather, it was accepted as a natural way of behaving in a world where the private and public realms were not sharply distinguished.

Change came, and continues to come, only where the bulk of the population begin to perceive authority relationships in a different way. Croatia is a good example of a society in transition between the old and the new modes of thought. When the city officials of Zagreb decided, within a year or two of the end of communism, to cut down many of the trees in their city, one very westernized commentator, Slavenka Drakulić, was outraged at the lack of consultation:

> No city bureaucrat would have dreamed of publicly discussing any sort of plan, much less delivering reports on, say, the public money spent on such a project . . . The administrators and the experts behave as though they are not responsible to anyone but the mayor, who gave them their jobs and who is paying them. The mayor of Zagreb has evidently not yet learned that he is responsible to the citizens . . .[5]

This state of mind Drakulić considered to be a hangover from communism. In fact, however, the 'communist mindset' was, in this respect, simply a modified form of pre-modernity; officials are personally answerable to their superior, not to abstractions such as 'the public'.

Slowly, Croats are changing. More and more of them are coming to share Drakulić's (that is, Western) expectations. The same process continues in much of the non-West today, though much, much more slowly than in Zagreb. The idea of 'personal' authority persists in most of the world, where corruption remains the cheapest form of taxation. It is so all-pervasive that it is very hard indeed to root out. What has mostly disappeared, however, is the personal state (personal, that is, at the apex of power) – even if the instincts that underlay it remain.

## The stability of pre-modern monarchies

Almost all pre-modern states (though the Roman Republic was a notable exception) were 'personal' in the sense that they were characterized by personal loyalty to a ruler whose rule was, likewise, personal. And if most humble subjects found king, prince or emperor impossibly remote, the intermediate layers of authority communicated loyalty of the same kind, both up and down the scale.

So although a king ruled personally, his personal hold upon his humbler and more far-flung subjects who had never met him – and never would meet him – was highly abstracted; it depended for its stability upon five elements: the maintenance of the personal ties along the length of the chain; the sustaining of the socially necessary myth of unity; the inculcation of fear, awe and deference to authority at every level; the hallowing of that authority with religious sanction; and the easy acceptance that only the long passage of time could provide.

Concerning the first of these elements, strong social discipline was imperative. The person who was disobedient to father or master or other figure of authority was, in a very real sense, challenging the entire basis of traditional society. To break the chain at one point was to threaten it at every point. 'If a man is an open rebel,' said Luther (rather incongruously, since Roman Catholics would have judged him as being pre-eminently guilty of precisely this) then 'every man is his judge and executioner, just as when a fire starts, the first to put it out is the best man.'[6] This is the continuing importance of respect and deference in much of the non-West today. The strong egalitarianism of the West cannot exist in the absence of Western hyper-prosperity, and the security that this hyper-prosperity provides. In its absence, security has to be provided by order. Western subversions of that order, through the cultural influences of film and TV, for example, seem to threaten anarchy.

That is why unity (the second element above) remains the supreme political virtue in much of the non-West, its maintenance vital, if only as a socially necessary façade. That is why, when pre-modern dissidents did emerge, they always insisted – and perhaps really believed – that they were not protesting against the monarch, but only against the actions inspired by his evil advisers. Luther, for example, tried to insist, at least during the early stage of his protest, that 'if the Pope knew the exactions of the preachers of Indulgences, he would rather have the basilica of St Peter reduced to ashes than built with the skin, flesh and bones of his sheep'.[7] Did he really believe this? Or was it just necessary for him to speak as though he did? It is perhaps not very meaningful to ask such questions. Similarly, the leaders of all religious factions at the time of the Reformation wrote as if they believed the various monarchs of Europe to be on their side even when evidence to support their assumptions was ambiguous or lacking, and occasionally even after evidence to the contrary had become irrefutable.

Wise monarchs, however, tried to give real substance to the myth of unity. All important factions needed to be represented at the highest levels of government; to exclude any of them was to drive them into opposition, and pre-modern states mostly lacked the resources to crush opposition except on an occasional basis. It was Charles I's mistake to forget this political reality, to sideline the Privy Council, to 'rule by favourites' and adopt a form of what would now be called 'conviction politics'. In so doing, he made the myth of unity unsustainable; the reality followed suit and his kingdoms collapsed into Civil War.

The ruler, in the pre-modern mind, has to be believed to be good by all his subjects and to have the interests of his people at heart. To admit the contrary would be either suicidal or else a call to arms in revolt, for to allow for the possibility of two irreconcilable claims co-existing in the body politic was ridiculous, since there were no mechanisms for accommodating them. So if a subject was unhappy with the ruler's actions, then it must be the fault of his advisers. This reflex habit of mind was still visible in twentieth-century Russia: when junior officials in the Soviet Union were confronted with the appalling consequences of communist policy, they convinced themselves that these were abuses happening without Stalin's knowledge.

Belief in unity is the reason that Third World major generals today, as they throw out the latest short-lived civilian administration in yet another military coup, so often defend themselves with the protestation that 'the politicians are all divided among themselves and cannot bring unity to this country'. To Westerners, the protestation seems ludicrous, for we 'know' that politicians are *supposed* to be divided, and that they are divided because we are. But we can afford to know this; we can afford to live with division and ambiguity in ways that the vast majority of humanity, who lived – and still live – close to the margins of existence, cannot. For them, all links of obedience and loyalty have to be kept strong, or else anarchy will follow.

In respect of the third element above, namely the inculcation of fear and awe, medieval kings in Europe seldom resided in one place; they were constantly touring from castle to castle, enforcing their rule with displays of power. The grand palaces and fortresses of other pre-modern monarchs, and the great public buildings of their Third World dictator–successors into the modern era, had – and have – the same purpose: to hold the subject in awe of the solidity of the ruler's power. The Ottoman sultans emphasized their solemn dignity – and gave visitors the creeps – by maintaining a rule of silence in the inner court:

> Visitors, told to wait hours in the second court, perceived that the walls were lined . . . with living men who never moved a muscle. The experience was almost hallucinatory, certainly unnerving. It was an expression, not merely of wealth, but of will.[8]

Purpose achieved.

As for the fourth ingredient above, the hallowing effect of religion, all pre-moderns understood that the basis of social order was rooted squarely in the numinous. Kings, fathers and husbands were to be obeyed because this was the will of God. The apostle Paul said so (although, in context, of course, qualifications were more than implied). Pre-modern kingdoms and empires allied themselves with religious faith. In Europe, they tended to prescribe the same one for all of their subjects, though the Romans before them, and the Chinese, Indians and at least some Muslim rulers, had the finer instinct of tolerating all religions that taught obedience while favouring one or another faith in particular. All religions claimed to give a final answer to any potential wise guy who might ask, 'Says who?' or 'Why should I?' – though the other features of pre-modern societies were such that, in practice, few characters of that sort ever emerged. If recent Western societies have witnessed a take-over by the wise guys and have demonstrated, to their own satisfaction at least, that it is possible to live without religion, it is because Western hyper-prosperity has made feasible meaningless lives propped up by vacuous play-acting and shallow entertainment. Most people have needed real meaning and, outside the West, they still do. They understand that an affront to piety is an assault on an entire society and the bonds that hold it together. It is a central aspect of their deep unease about Western influences on their societies. For Westerners act on the assumption that religion is a personal preference – and an irrational one at that.

Finally, pre-moderns understood that legitimacy rests upon reflex action more than upon the conscious will to submit, for, if one has to think very much or very often about the act of submitting, one is much more likely to choose – sometime, at least – to rebel. In such contexts, the permission of a journalistic media that makes its living by making our government and its policies the subject of 'a daily referendum'[9] is not invigorating, but insane; the 'cloistered virtue' at which Milton scoffed seems actually preferable.

In so far as the laws do have the unthinking obedience of the people who live under them, however, it is mostly because they have been around for a long time; this much is true of Western democracies and of non-democratic regimes and kingships alike. And none of the non-democratic regimes is more vulnerable than during the first few years after the rulers have seized power, for the simple reason that they lack the legitimacy that only the passage of time can supply. For this reason, in pre-modern societies, unless one had a clear vested interest in change and a well-founded belief in its likely success, then one had an even clearer vested interest in maintaining the status quo, for any change could be achieved only by violence and upheaval. All of which is to say what we knew anyway: pre-modern societies were – and are – inherently conservative.

# Imagined communities

One useful coinage of recent years is the expression 'imagined communities'. It is used mostly by historians of nationalism – or rather, of the development of national consciousness during recent centuries. The term refers to the groups to which people perceive themselves as 'belonging'. My 'imagined community' is the 'we' or 'us' of which I instinctively and primarily consider myself to be a part. The others in this 'community' need not necessarily be 'like me' in a sense that would satisfy today's protagonists of identity politics, for they will, at a minimum, include my family, which automatically spans both sexes and more than one generation. They will be those with whom I unreflectively (and that is the key word) consider myself, my interests and my destiny to be bound up. They will be those whom I mean when I use an ill-considered 'we'.

For pre-modern people – and for many Third World people even today – the 'imagined community' was the district or region, not the kingdom or 'state' to which the district happened (for the time being) to belong. What kept a pre-modern state together was the personal authority of its ruler, mediated to his lowliest subjects by a chain of strong, intermediate institutions, bigger than the individual or family, but smaller than the kingdom – that is, precisely those institutions that modernist political discourse of both

Right and Left has destroyed – mostly centring on personal loyalties. In this way, most states consisted of several – or perhaps many – 'imagined communities'.

Precisely because pre-modern states did not – and do not – constitute 'a people', most ordinary folk were indifferent as to who was their king. If their province was transferred by treaty or by warfare to the rule of another monarch, the fact made no difference to their lives one way or the other. The ordinary person's loyalties were, on the micro-level, to locality and its traditions and to particular families. On the macro-level, they were to the large entity (say, 'Christendom') to which all such localities as he or she had cognizance of belonged. A thirteenth-century French peasant, forced to identify himself to time-travellers from the early twenty-first century, would have been unlikely to claim to be 'French' or 'a peasant' – though he might possibly have confessed to either of these if pressed by his interrogators. He would describe himself firstly as a 'Christian' (by which he would mean that he was not a Muslim or a Turk) and secondly as the subject of such-and-such a local lord, or perhaps as the inhabitant of a particular region. A rural Algerian might do the equivalent even today: first a 'Muslim', then an inhabitant of a certain village or district. The Russian word for 'peasant' – *krest'ian*, or 'Christian' – tells its own story. As Richard Pipes observes:

> The Russian peasant of 1900 owed loyalty only to his own village and canton; at most he was conscious of some vague allegiance to his province. His sense of national identity was confined to respect for the Tsar and suspicion of foreigners.[1]

To move from this situation to the circumstance of the modern state, it has been necessary for the shape and size of the 'imagined community' to change, so that it is no longer the village or province, but is instead coterminous with the state. It has become necessary for people to think of themselves, not primarily as Devonians, but primarily as English and, later, British; not first and foremost as Thuringians, but first and foremost as Germans; not mainly as Slavonians but mainly as Croats (their failure to visualize themselves as Yugoslavs spelt the doom of the state once *vox populi* counted for anything). This process took place at different rates. In many parts of the world, it is far from complete and, in some cases, it has barely started.

The fact that the Habsburg Empire was not the 'imagined community' of most ordinary people in Slavonia, for example, was not problematic (at least until national consciousness became prominent there during the nineteenth century), because the Empire was glued together by strong intermediate loyalties that bound each peasant to his lord, and each lord to his *župan* or *vojvod*, and each *župan* and *vojvod* to the royal court. Something broadly similar was true of almost all pre-modern states. But the coming of modernity – and especially mass urbanization – changes the picture. For this dissolves many of the intermediate loyalties on which pre-modern states depend. People who live in large cities do not see themselves as 'the subject of Lord Frederick', nor are they. Their regional loyalties may endure, if the city is not too large and is the centrepiece of a city–state. But in the end, they will see the 'imagined community' to which they belong as people like themselves.

And who, once I have become urbanized and detached from hereditary ties of district and extended family, is 'like me'? Who is the 'we' to whom I now belong? Will it be someone who shares my language? Or will it be someone who shares the same religious faith? The industrial revolution opened a third possible 'imagined community' – mass-urbanized populations began to speak of social 'classes', whose members might share solidarity.

## *Religion*

In point of fact, however, most nationalist intellectuals preferred the criterion of language; 'religion' was too much
bound up with the business of supporting the old-style, personal rulers. Religious leaders during the eighteenth and
nineteenth centuries were usually fierce opponents of
nationalism (though Serbia was an exception). It was only
after the First World War, when the Habsburg Empire and
the Ottoman Empire had been dissolved and new
'nation–states' established, that religion became more
prominent in discriminating against minorities, or forcing
sharp divisions between (say) Serbs and Croats. Likewise, it
was only with the final collapse of the old monarchies in the
early twentieth century that the Roman Catholic Church
was forced to choose between the only political rivals that
modernity suffered to exist. The Church's preferred form of
government (preferred, that is, since 1648), namely absolutist monarchy, was everywhere in its death throes, where
it had not already been extinguished. The Habsburgs and
the lesser princelings were no more. The industrial states
and republicanism had triumphed. It was only at that point
that nationalism came to be seen no longer as the creed of
upstart urbanites and budding parliamentarians, but as the
least bad defence against the sinful, distasteful liberal–
democratic society or, yet more horrifying, the spectre of
godless Bolshevism. *Mutatis mutandis*, the Orthodox
churches of eastern Europe faced similar choices and came
to similar conclusions. Thus it was only in the twentieth
century that some nationalisms (though not that of the
Nazis) took on a distinctly religious hue, where before they
had been distinctly secular and anti-clerical.

In the predominantly Protestant UK and USA, the
ever-changing kaleidoscope of evangelical sectarianism
flourished during the nineteenth century and did indeed help
to convey identity, meaning and purpose to the newly

uprooted souls whom the heartless process of industrialization had wrenched from the soil into urban anonymity. But, precisely because it was sectarian, the identity conveyed was personal and private (albeit with public effects) rather than political; by the nature of the case, there could be no attempt to establish a Methodist or Baptist state. The nearest approach was a generalized cultural hegemony, fleetingly achieved around the mid-nineteenth century and shared by the coalition as a whole. It never challenged the concept of national identity.

In practice, then, the three possible rivals reduced themselves, in Western countries, to just two. Religion and language were both subsumed into the 'imagined community' of 'nation'. 'Nation' and 'class' vied for the allegiance of people in the new, urban mass societies.

## Nation

National awareness developed apace. The eighteenth century saw the feverish production of dictionaries and encyclopaedias, of grammar books and philological studies. These were less an exercise in dispassionate scholarship than attempts to claim some particular dialect as a standard to which the others ought to conform, or to draw the boundaries of a language in such a way as to claim the population of a particular area as 'really' belonging to one nation rather than to another.

What, in the long run, determined the difference between a language and a dialect was disarmingly simple: a language was a dialect with an army. Thus it was that some scholars in the early nineteenth century 'doubted the existence of Croat linguistic distinctiveness'; even in the early twentieth century, poems in Kajkavski (the dialects spoken around Zagreb) were included in Karol Štrekelj's *Slovenske Narodne Pesmi* ('Slovene Folk Songs'). In rural Slovenia, meanwhile, dialects varied so much that, 'before the language was codified, simple communication was all that was possible between valleys'.[2] The continuities between Dutch and *Deutsch* before the modern period were, to put the matter mildly, striking; early sixteenth-century English people referred to all of the dialects spoken in the Netherlands and north Germany under the term 'base Almayne', and a glance at a Lübeck Bible from, say, the 1530s is enough to see why. It was only in 1945 that Tito's Communists designated Macedonian as a 'language' distinct from both Bulgarian and Serbo-Croat (the latter since dissipated, of course, into Serbian and Croatian by force of arms). Examples could be multiplied endlessly.

Where dialects have had minimal support from 'armies' (that is, from state machineries), they continue to struggle to become standardized languages, even today. 'Standard Welsh' remains a rather self-conscious affair, almost unknown in the home, and which has to be taught even to Welsh-speakers through school and television; the dialects continue to reign supreme. Obviously, such fuzziness between dialect and language only holds within a given language group; the boundaries between Croatian and Hungarian, say, or between German and Italian, are pretty self-evident. Nevertheless, within those constraints it remains true to say that, in linguistic matters, the 'imagined community' of the nation is precisely that: a political construct, not a *datum*.

The failure of ordinary people to see themselves as belonging to the 'nation' to which urban nationalists wished to assign them was a cause of perplexity and distress to the latter.

As the geographer Jovan Cvijić noted, the Slavs in the southern Morava valley had 'a very vague national consciousness' before 1878, and were only taught to think of themselves as Serbs thereafter. Slav speakers in the Kosovo region would refer to their language simply as

*naš jezik* or *naški*, 'our language'; if they were members
of the Serbian Orthodox Church they would call themselves Serbs, but this was a religious identification more
than a national one. Much effort was made by the
Serbian consuls and Serbian-trained schoolteachers to
instil a 'national' consciousness into these people. As late
as 1912, one scandalised report by Milojević (who had
become Serbian consul in Priština) said that some of the
Serbs of Mitrovica were identifying themselves not as
Serbians but as 'Kosovci', Kosovans. . . .

Serbian diplomats began to be irritated by the
degree of Russian interference in Kosovo: one junior
consular official, the talented young writer Milan
Rakić, noted in 1905 that Serb villagers in the Dečani
region were beginning to describe themselves, absurdly,
as Russians.[3]

Even today, many non-nationalistic (or merely prudent)
inhabitants of Bosnia continue to refer to their tongue, cau-
tiously, simply as 'our language' – though now the phrase is
not so much an expression of innocence as of wariness
about the implications of calling it anything at all.

National self-consciousness is still a fairly recent import
into Slavic space. Before the Bolshevik Revolution of 1917,
it was predominantly an urban affair.

Pre-revolutionary literary sources similarly stress the
absence among the peasantry of belonging to the state
or nation. They depict it as insulated from influences
external to the village and lacking in awareness of
national identity. Tolstoy emphatically denied the
peasant a sense of patriotism: I have never heard any
expression of patriotic sentiments from the people, but,
on the contrary . . . the most absolute indifference or
even contempt for all kinds of manifestations of patriotism. The truth of this observation was demonstrated

> during World War I, when the Russian peasant soldier
> . . . did not understand why he was fighting since the
> enemy did not threaten his home province.[4]

The nineteenth century saw, in the West, the production of 'national' anthems and hymns, the digging out of folklore and the design of allegedly traditional (but in fact mostly new-fangled) 'national' costumes and the production of flags. In the non-West, these things have mostly been undertaken only during the twentieth century, because the form of national consciousness on which they are predicated has only lately been imported from the West. In all cases, however, the production of such cultural emblems has not so much *reflected* popular national consciousness as been an instrument (by those who already possessed it) to *create* such consciousness in the masses of the population who did not possess it. Both the degree and the rate of success have varied from one state to another, and also within states.

Many states have continued, as a matter of course, to create homogeneity by minimizing or understating the numbers of ethnic minority populations and to attempt forcible assimilation to the nationalists' 'norm'. During the twentieth century this has been done by using the levers of state: education (for example, in Wales and Catalonia), registration of names (for example, in Greek Macedonia and Brittany), official media (almost everywhere). At its most brutal and savage, the philosophy was expressed by the fascist Ustaše regime in Nazi-occupied Croatia vis-à-vis the Serbs: kill a third, convert a third, expel a third. Thankfully, most would-be nation–states have employed much less extreme measures than this, but the overall goal of homogeneity – that is, of forcing the real community to conform to the imagined one – remained the same.

## Class

In the emerging, modern Western world, the rival new 'imagined community' to that of nation was 'class'. Socialists were not keen on feelings of national solidarity, for that would entail fellow-feeling between factory workers and their employers. (Though in fairness it should be said that where, as in much of central and eastern Europe, the bourgeois were of a different language or religion to the proletariat, socialist agitators were not above exploiting the fact.) Primarily, socialists wanted industrial workers to feel solidarity with one another, rather than with their ethnic kin. Only a political movement oriented primarily towards class, rather than around linguistic or religious loyalties, could bring in socialism. This rivalry for the loyalty of the new urban populations was expressed quite consciously in the famous last line of the *Communist Manifesto*: 'Working men of all countries, unite!' Never mind your nationality; membership of the proletariat was what mattered. The point of their anthem, 'The Internationale', was the same.

Marx, of course, contended that 'the history of all hitherto-existing societies is the history of class struggle'. This absurd claim is the equivalent, for socialism, of what Mel Gibson's film *Braveheart* is for nationalism: the projection back on to the past of forms of consciousness that would have been almost incomprehensible to the real inhabitants of that past. In representation, at least, the real past is made to conform to the imagined present. But in the real present, socialists and nationalists alike expended a very large proportion of their energies in persuading their unwilling beneficiaries of who they (the beneficiaries) 'really were'.

In the modern era, 'nation' and 'class' were united only in their rejection of the real 'imagined communities' of the pre-modern world, namely district and personal loyalties, and of the personal monarchies that had depended upon them.

This rivalry – 'class' versus 'nation' – was fought out on

a gigantic scale during the first half of the twentieth century. Nationalists fought Communists in the Spanish Civil War, with the former gaining the victory. The conflict between Chiang Kai-shek's Nationalists and Mao's Communists in the Chinese civil war, however, produced the opposite result. Nationalist and Communist movements vied for the allegiance of electorates across Europe, their contests constantly threatening to spill over into violence. In the titanic battle between Nazi Germany and the Soviet Union, the struggle between the 'imagined communities' of nation and class was at the very heart of the Second World War – and of almost all the de facto civil wars that continued to be fought out under the blanket of Nazi occupation. If 'class' appeared to win over 'nation', it should be remembered that the demise of communism in 1989–90 was accompanied by an upsurge in national and tribal–religious feeling across eastern Europe; even the erstwhile 'working masses' needed to know who, apart from being proletarians, they now were.

## Changing states and the non-Western crisis of legitimacy

Compared with all of this, the pre-modern world had been blissfully free of ideologies. Then, all politics had been personal. There were no 'political programmes'; in any case, no government had been strong enough or possessed of enough resources to have – except in the vaguest and most ineffectual of senses – 'a policy'. For these reasons, all political conflicts had been personal, too; they were nothing more than naked struggles for power.

Medieval monarchs had commanded the personal allegiance of their subjects. Indeed, this conception is present in the very idea of a 'subject'; the person so described is, literally, subjected to the will, or rule, of his liege lord. Under feudalism each person was bound, in hereditary ties of fealty and protection reinforced by solemn oaths, to a lord above him and to subjects below him, in a pyramid with its summit in the person of the monarch. Not all pre-modern societies made the ties explicit in this way, but the effect was broadly similar. The subjects of a prince, a king or an emperor were bound by ties that were personal. They were not even quite territorial. Demarcation of frontiers was, so to speak, secondary to the ties of allegiance. The arrangement was but one stage removed from the tribal situation, where precise areas of settlement might be subject to change without altering the political bonds of the group. This phenomenon is still seen in parts of central Asia, where frontiers mean little and tribes mean everything. Even where medieval and pre-modern frontiers were fixed, however, they expressed the limits of a sovereign's sovereignty; they did not describe nor constitute a 'people'. Kingdoms, principalities, duchies, empires, khanates, margravates: all were coterminous with the power of kings, princes, dukes, emperors, khans and margraves. Some such states were – and are – actually named for their ruling families or founders; so we have the Habsburg Empire, Saudi Arabia, or the Ottoman realm (named for Osman).

Accordingly, the frontiers of pre-modern states were seldom coterminous with the 'imagined communities' of their populations. Speakers of different languages mingled easily enough together. The apparatus of state was so light, and government impinged so little on everyday life, that the language of the ruling caste was seldom a threat to differing tongues among subject peoples – and in any case the latter rarely had the strong sense of group solidarity that might render such situations a political problem.

Religion might be more difficult, especially in Christian Europe, with populations required by their rulers to conform. But this was largely because the rulers were themselves subject to the papacy, which demanded rigour from Roman Catholic monarchs; the altar was stronger than the throne. Religion in Europe was a necessary, but not a sufficient, condition for political legitimacy.

Political legitimacy in the pre-modern world depended mostly on the combination of power and tradition. If a dynasty was forcibly replaced, the new ruler would be seen as a usurper and would need to maintain his rule by mainforce and threats of violence for his own lifetime, as perhaps might his successor. But when a polity had been in place for many years, tradition was mostly enough to make it legitimate, and force could afford to drift into the background.

But even invasion could be accepted with equanimity once the initial shock of a change in rulers had passed. Precisely because the old kingdom had not been the 'imagined community' of its population, the invaded did not feel that their selfhood was being imposed on, or that they were somehow the victims of a sort of collective political rape. If the new rulers did not tamper too much, or too suddenly, with the existing mechanisms of life at the local level, then the real 'imagined communities' of the invaded remained intact.

It is this kind of stability that the intrusion of modernity from the West has destroyed. It does not take much effort of imagination to realize that the Afghan monarchy in the 1970s oversaw far greater stability in Afghanistan than did the modernist alternatives since the Soviet invasion. It thereby maintained much greater security for ordinary people – which, as Hobbes has taught us, is the first requirement of any state. The king upheld stability by the simple fact that his legitimacy was accepted by all the various tribes and language groups, because of tradition. The communists tried to replace this with a spurious class-based state, and won the implacable resistance of most of the population. The Taliban attempted a narrow confessionalist regime (which was in any case, a cover for the dominance of one tribe). Both communists and Taliban relied entirely upon force – and failed even then – because they were not perceived as legitimate. The Western powers now wish to impose democracy and the creation of an impersonal nation–state at the point of a gun. It will be interesting to see if they succeed. (At the time of writing, all the signs are that it won't; the Western-backed government's writ does not run outside Kabul.)

The tragedy of much of the non-West is that its states are mostly in a constant crisis of legitimacy. The Europeans' colonial empires destroyed and absorbed the traditional kingdoms and states of the non-West. They could not simply be re-assembled once those empires themselves fell apart after the Second World War. 'The Divine Right of Kings' or its variants can no more be recreated than we can bring back Neanderthal man. Monarchies, once gone and abolished for more than a few years, cannot be resurrected, except perhaps as ceremonial ornaments. The states of the non-West, the creations of revolution, recent war or de-colonization, are forced instead to adopt all the forms and paraphernalia of the modern state – impersonal institutions, public health and education services, presidential govern-ment – while their populations still have the instinctive habits of personal authority and localized allegiances. Unsurprisingly, some of them disintegrate and become what the po-faced Western media piously call 'failed states'. Afghanistan is one example; Somalia is another; Congo (Zaire) is yet another. Lebanon has been painfully recon-structed, though at the price of Syrian occupation. Several other states, though not exactly 'failed', have nevertheless not been in full control of their theoretical territory for decades on end; the names of Sudan and Myanmar (Burma) come to mind.

The very frontiers of many of the new states, some of which are mere straight lines drawn on maps by colonial administrators, often bear little resemblance to the de facto 'imagined communities' of their populations. Of 132 states existing back in 1971, only 12 could be considered genuine nation–states, and in 39 cases the largest ethnic group made up less than 50 per cent of the population of its state.[5] Governments in such situations are practically forced to whip up nationalist enthusiasm artificially as the only alternative to tribalism, regionalism and the fragmentation of the state. That is to say, they try to create new 'imagined communities' that are coterminous with the frontiers of the state. Slowly, they are succeeding. The Soviet empire and Yugoslavia failed spectacularly and disintegrated into closer approximations to 'nation–states' (though it is by no means clear that the process is yet entirely finished). Elsewhere, urban populations gradually come to see themselves as, for example, Zimbabweans first and as Shona only after that. Rural populations, however, change much more slowly; there is little that might persuade the Karen people (to take one of the most painful examples) to see themselves as Burmese.

Where national identity is slow to catch on, or where it cannot easily be squared with the frontiers of the state, an important rival has emerged: religion. Here again, Western expectations are confounded by actual events:

> The reach of the modern and postmodern worldviews, extended through the impact of globalization, has not weakened the influence of religion in non-Western societies as had been commonly anticipated in the West. They are, rather, having the opposite effect. Religion is strengthening its public role and is providing inspiration for resisting Western universalism and plurality.[6]

It was this that led to the partition of India in 1947, with a million dead and seven million refugees: the price of creating states in (very imperfect) accordance with the 'imagined community' of religious affiliation. It continues to strengthen 'Hindu nationalism'. In the Islamic world, it also remains a very powerful idea, building as it does on the ancient concept of the *ummah* – the Muslim people of the world as a whole. For this reason, radical Islamists often consider the states in which they actually live to be illegitimate and intrinsically secular; only the 'imagined community' of the *ummah* can form a political unit. Such ideas appeal strongly to the first and second generation of urban dwellers, just as did the Methodist Church and the Baptist Church in industrializing nineteenth-century Great Britain and the USA. But whereas evangelical sectarianism was personalized and politically neutral – or even stabilizing – Islamism is destabilizing because it calls into question the legitimacy of existing states.

Democracy cannot exist for any length of time where there is little correspondence between a state's frontiers and the 'imagined communities' of those who live in them. Although it is a fact often repeated that the number of democracies in the world has shot up sharply since the end of the Cold War, those democracies are in most cases more apparent than real, and few endure for more than one or two tenures of office. The only Third World state that has succeeded in maintaining a pattern of democratic elections for a prolonged period (indeed, since 1948) is India – and even that example is badly flawed in practice. For most states, the only alternative to legitimacy is force.

As Huntington has tried to tell us, Third World states are unlikely to remain democracies in anything but the most formal of senses, and the more their governments are genuinely vulnerable to popular pressure, the more likely they are to repress their minorities – whether linguistic or religious (or, as in India, social) – and to adopt strident anti-Westernism. If Mubarak or the house of ibn Sa'ud are overthrown, as looks entirely likely, it will not be because of their 'failure to respect human rights', but because they have failed sufficiently to reflect the Islamist sentiments of their teeming urban populations. The Christian minorities of Egypt and Syria have everything to fear from the fall of the Mubarak and Assad regimes.

It is the failure of the Western imagination to confront the most obvious cultural realities about the world on its doorstep – or even about its own past – that is driving its relationship with the remaining 90 per cent of the global population into a corner. By refusing – or, at any rate, failing – to understand, co-existence becomes impossible, and the only possible bases for relationship between West and non-West are those of domination or collision. Domination has succeeded until now. But it is starting to come badly unstuck and clearly cannot endure. The choices facing the West during the coming century are not between decline and continued domination. They are between gradual, managed decline and catastrophic conflict. We are presently embarked on the latter course.

It is not that the former choice, that of managed decline, could ever leave us entirely free of violence; freedom from having to make lethal choices is no more a possibility for us than it was in the world of Machiavelli. Fighting terrorist groups and the taking on of regimes that supply them may be necessary to keep body counts down. Hand-wringing inaction fuelled by self-loathing (itself a classic symptom of the anti-culture) is a recipe for certain mega-death. The terrorists are not motivated by wealth discrepancies, nor even (except in an immediate, precipitative sense) by Western foreign policies. Consequently it is quite certain that no concessions in those areas – except perhaps the ludicrous one of trying to evacuate Israel of its entire population – could ever appease them. In any case, in the absence of business cultures and political arrangements to match, no transfers of wealth would do any good.

The long-term path away from catastrophic conflict is to be sought elsewhere. It is to be found by refraining from the cultural imperialism presently being inflicted on the non-West by our anti-culture and its anti-values. And, you know, to stop it happening there, we really have to tackle it here.

# Divided lives, infantilized culture

Introductory books and teaching materials on missiology or anthropology or the history of some non-Western area of the world never fail to make me laugh. There will be a few introductory paragraphs, describing the general features of the country or people group to be discussed – and then there will be an earnest, po-faced explanation to the student or initiate that 'family is very important to the Mbongo people' or that 'Chinese culture is highly collectivist' or that the 'swamp-dwelling Mudscratchers put the needs of their community above personal preferences'. Such facts are presented in a way that implies that this is somehow a noteworthy distinctive of the people about to be studied. Perhaps it is less painful to the audience to speak this way, and to allow the truly shocking realization, namely that only one culture has ever thought or acted in any other fashion, to remain, like the truth about Father Christmas, an undiscovered, dreadful secret. (It will be appreciated that I am assuming no readers of this book who are under the age of ten will have progressed this far!)

Timothy McDaniel's admirably incisive account of Russian social and political attitudes notes that the traditional peasant village was not noted for its tolerance of Jews, foreigners, or people of other faiths. Non-married people were looked upon as only partly human. Women had their defined and subordinate place in peasant society, and age was also an extremely important marker of status hierarchy.[1]

He might have been describing the general tendencies of almost any pre-modern or non-Western society.

When did we Westerners start to change into individualists, and why? The answer is almost certainly to be found in the Industrial Revolution. It was that development which created the wholesale phenomenon of 'going out to work', an arrangement that has now been so ubiquitous for so long that most Westerners assume it to be part of the order of nature. When manufacturing machinery became too large to be accommodated in a worker's cottage, then the factory ceased to be an exceptional institution and became the rule. So too did 'going out to work'.

This development has had a radical impact on the family. Instead of being an economic unit of production, with family life centred around work in which all participated, it became instead a place of consumption. The worker went 'out', away from the home, to work, and 'brought home the bacon'. More usually, the 'bacon' was metaphorical; the Industrial Revolution was an important stage in the shift to a cash economy.

The new, industrial family may have been far more vulnerable than its pre-industrial forebears, but it was also far more flexible. Land, or a place in a trade, had never been simply 'out there' for the asking in the pre-industrial world. Geographical mobility had been the exception, not the rule. Families had stayed put. But in the new, industrial world, the worker who left his or her home each morning to go to a factory might do so equally well in one place as in another. The very design and location of the new industrial enterprises created mobility among the populations who worked in them. Attachment to place and to extended family began to ebb away. Vast numbers of Irish people moved to England and Wales – or to America. Country people moved to the towns.

The family was no longer a unit of production, but a home base from which its various members sallied forth each day to work (and, after the introduction of compulsory education, to school) in different locations. They came home at night to share the spoils that had been earned during the day. The family was thereby reoriented from production to consumption. The potential, as the population grew more prosperous, for the consumer society had been created.

So too had a sharp division between private and public worlds. Before the Industrial Revolution, such distinctions had been almost invisible. One's family formed the core of who one was. Except for soldiers away on campaign, it was scarcely possible for ordinary people to form friendships – or any relationships at all – that did not embroil one's immediate relatives at a very early stage. The re-creation of workplace as public space altered all of that. Work (and, for children, school) were now part of the public world. One operated there independently of one's family. One could form friendships (in large cities, at least) in which one's family had no involvement whatsoever.

When young people meet as colleagues in the office today, or as students at college, or in the anonymity of a bar or night club, the very last thing on their minds is whether their new acquaintance is 'from a good family', or what their parents do for a living, or whether they have any family at all. The family has been relegated to a separate, private domain, a matter of personal choice (or, more likely these days, of embarrassment). One is friends with the person, not with his or her relatives. The fact that this new mentality remains dominant even once a friendship becomes very serious ('I'm marrying you, not your mother!') is indicative of the weakening of extended family, even where the nuclear family survives.

The moral dangers of urbanization – in the increased fragility of the family and the weakening of restraints on individual behaviour – were recognized even before the Industrial Revolution made urban existence the norm. Medieval churchmen and monks had fulminated against the peculiar 'sinfulness' of the city. However exaggerated their attachments to feudal solidarity, and however laughable and repulsive to us their horror at the way in which towns-people escaped its tyranny, the ecclesiastics nevertheless saw, in a sense, truly. They perceived correctly that the anonymity of town life reduced the accountability of individual behaviour. It enabled anybody and everybody (in principle, at least) to make a living from whomever and whatever would employ them. For precisely these reasons, town life was the first recourse of minorities – Jews in Europe, Armenians in the Ottoman realms, Chinese in South Asia – because those who stood outside of the estab-lished structures of power could continue to live, and even thrive, without the approval of those structures.

We have come a long way since those times. Yet the dynamics remain the same. And those dynamics continue to fill the guardians of tradition in non-Western societies with deep unease. It was for reasons like these that the Victor-ians, members of the first industrial society, guaranteed themselves against social and moral anarchy by emphasiz-ing what Burke called the 'controlling power upon will and appetite . . . within'. As noted earlier, however, the internal policeman has since been dismissed, and we are now faced with the consequences.

## *The inevitable fragility of the post-modern family*

The way of working produced by the Industrial Revolution was more efficient, since it allowed workers to move to where they were needed (and then move on again as needs changed), untrammelled by ties of extended family and locality. As family was increasingly disregarded by firms and public institutions when they made their appointments, significant social mobility resulted; it became much easier to leave behind one's lowly social origins and rise up the scale on the strength of one's own achievements. This process enhanced both personal freedoms and the efficiency of the economy – which is to say that the 'good of the individual' and the 'good of everyone' combined to whittle down the importance of the intermediate-sized institutions, such as family.

'Family' is a consideration which has come to belong more and more 'indoors'. It is none of the employer's business. And, during the hours that he or she is in work, it is none of the employee's business, either. Personal allegiances have no place in the public world. The family, then, has become, in the modern West, a mere private concern. By the same token, so, too, has sexual behaviour. Whether the man selling me a washing machine is married, homosexual, celibate, lives with a girlfriend or cruises the streets each night looking for action is none of my concern. Such a state of mind would have been inconceivable in any society but ours.

The privacy of the family also makes it far more fragile. In a pre-modern world, where my livelihood, my marriage and my standing in the only community to which I ever could, realistically, belong are entirely bound up together, then marriage bonds will be strong also. Social solidarity serves to reinforce them. Where survival from one year to the next can never be taken for granted, the establishment of a viable home and the raising of at least some children to adulthood will count as a successful marriage.

But in a society where I can re-invent my life in an anony-mous pea-soup of people, change my career, move home and make new friends in a different place, marriage bonds will be weakened. This was hardly an option open to pre-modern people. Quite apart from the laws and the more powerful force of social disapproval, the very material realities of life conspired against it. Moving away and re-inventing one's life from scratch was not an option unless one was happy to submit to beggary. For precisely this reason, of course, such irregularity of marital and domestic life as did appear was almost always among the beggar class; they had little or nothing to lose. (At the opposite extreme, kings and the very great could experiment with promiscuity, and much less frequently with irregular mar-riage arrangements; their power enabled them to withstand the resultant strain.) For ordinary people, the necessities of life were best guaranteed by strong family ties.

Where the 'glue' that holds the marriage together is no longer the self-interest of survival (for even moderate pros-perity can be taken for granted nowadays) but rather the ability to enjoy the same entertainments together for half a century, then the edifice of the family is more prone to come apart. The pre-industrial – and even the industrial – family was bound together by common participation in the almost superhuman struggle to make a decent life, or to survive at all. The post-industrial family, secure in the essentials of life, with plenty of time on its hands and no economic functions intrinsic to itself, is more likely to get bored with one another's company.

The post-modern family has at once too much and too little demanded of it. Too much, because it is now required to provide emotional fulfilment and stimulation across a lifetime – which is harsh when we consider that the emotions of its constituent members (I speak, of course, of ourselves) are not consistent or necessarily compatible with those of anyone else, for even minutes together. Yet that is now the basis for family life. Too little is demanded of the family because its function in providing economic security is now greatly diminished; it is, strictly speaking, unnecessary. At the bottom end of society, security has been socialized through the State. (Patricia Morgan's studies have shown that the presence of a father is an economic liability to a mother, rather than an asset, if those concerned are living on welfare.[2]) At the top end, although high earners can provide an incentive to their families to stick with them, they are yet simultaneously vulnerable to hefty divorce settlements; many high-earners cite this as a reason for not marrying at all, and it is undoubtedly a factor in the trend towards 'pre-nuptial agreements' (as we have learned to call them) among the most prosperous.

The long-term emotional entertainment that families are now required to provide is particularly hard when we consider that the average length of those marriages that do stay together is in any case far longer than it used to be. Fifty years or more can now be expected. When life spans were shorter, a busy, effort-filled 20–30 years was closer to the average. In that earlier world, even troubled marriages might be resolved naturally, so to speak.

In the light of all this, Christian preachments about the importance of marriage and the family will be an uphill struggle. Yes, our society is certainly more immoral in this area than any other society has been. But even if we can cut out pornography and abortion, or desexualize our social environment (prospects that, it should be said, look quite beyond us at the moment), we cannot go back to a mythical Merrie England or Plymouth Plantation. The social consequences of the Industrial Revolution cannot be undone. Even if we could (in part, at least) reinstate the safeguards of the nineteenth century, we cannot go back further than that.

## *The sexualization of society*

But can we reinstate the safeguards even of the nineteenth century? That the fragmentation of family, the anonymity of mass-urban life and the radicalized division between public and private worlds should lead to an increase in sexual immorality should by now be obvious.

But several other factors have also contributed towards it. In the first place, rising living standards have greatly reduced the age of puberty. The often-cited example of Shakespeare's *Romeo and Juliet* has led many people to suppose that 14 was a very usual age of puberty in the pre-modern world. In fact, however, nothing could be further from the truth. Lady Capulet was from the most privileged, best-fed section of her society, and puberty at such a young age was an indication of it.[3] Even then, one suspects, she would have been an unusual person in this respect.

The reality for ordinary folk was very different. There are two reasons for this: insufficient wealth and late sexual maturity. In the first place, most young people in the early-modern period were 'put into service' in late childhood (that is, they went to work as servants in the household of someone richer, since their parents either could not support them or wished to help them make their way in the world). This was particularly true in towns. Young people often could not marry until they had served their long apprentice-ships or come into enough money to establish households of their own.

In the second place, most people subsisted on a much poorer diet than ours. Remember the low doors in old buildings? People in the past were much shorter than we are; the average height of Westerners has been increasing by a centimetre a decade since the mid-nineteenth century. The average height of the British soldier at Waterloo in 1815 was 5 foot 2 inches (157 cm) – and they made fun of the 'starveling Frenchies', who were, on average, worse fed and physically feebler! Sexual maturity was often not reached until late teens or even later. In the 1850s, country girls in Norway often did not reach puberty until their late teens, and even in the years before the First World War recruits to the Austro-Hungarian Emperor's army who came from Bukovina were constantly having to be sent home again because, at the age of 20 or 21, their voices hadn't broken and they remained, physically, boys. In places where the age of sexual maturity was indeed closer to ours, such as in parts of southern Europe, then early marriage was the norm.[4] Early marriage, of course, is hardly the norm with modern Westerners. The adolescent and young adult experience is now typified by lots of sexual urges rushing around and no marriage partner to enjoy them with. The results are not entirely surprising.

Furthermore, the reduced age of puberty has coincided with a greatly increased age at which young people come to be useful, productive members of society. Few now contribute to the economy or have any real responsibilities placed on them before their late teens at the earliest. Among the ever-increasing minority (especially in the middle classes) who go to university or college, non-productive life is extended, via the odd gap year and drop-out years, well into the early 20s and even, in Germany, to the mid-20s. As recently as two generations ago, this was very different. The process of including young people in the productive economy when scarcely out of childhood served to bind them into work disciplines and to create a far stronger link between personal behaviour and its consequences. Now, there are lots of hormones and sex urges sloshing around and nothing (nothing, that is, if traditional morality is to be adhered to) to do with them. Unsurprisingly, the thing that 'gives' in this situation is traditional morality.

The search for a mate was a mainstay of literature, art and music in very many cultures. But in the extended adolescence of Western countries, art has portrayed life as an extended series of amours; the hormones have to have somewhere to go, and marriage is hardly an option if one is serious about pursuing higher education or the mobile career that follows it. The promiscuity that (mostly) results, however, simply heightens our sense of insecurity and reduces our sense of self-worth.

Wendy Shalit has masterfully chronicled this process at work in her study of popular culture among young women. In particular, she highlights the value of sexual modesty, and chronicles the catastrophic results that abandoning it has on our mental health.

> I realize some say that embarrassment is socially con-structed, and that's a part of it, but I don't think it's the main part. I would say the opposite – that embarrass-ment is natural but it can be socially *de*structed . . . Embarrassment is actually a wonderful signal, namely, that something isn't quite right . . . Embarrassment is silly, but the fact is, it is also what makes girls strong . . . Taught from day one that we should always give in to the animal, and that our embarrassment is a problem – '*now remember boys and girls, there is absolutely nothing to giggle about!*' – girls today have nothing to protect what is human in them . . . Stripped of their natural embarrassment, girls are only more vulnerable: they just give in – again and again.
>
> Yet the human soul ends up reasserting itself, anyway, only since this time the disparity is between what they hoped for and what they got, the result is not embarrassment or hesitation, but usually misery – and that's when they start cutting themselves up. Misery because there is no longer anything they can do about it. At least when there is embarrassment or discomfort, that points to *not* doing something. Thus, Kelli, a 15-year-old patient of Mary Pipher's, asks her psychologist: 'Did my mom tell you we were having sex?' When Dr

Pipher nods, the girl hastens to add, 'It's no big deal,'
because she is, of course, 'on the Pill.' And yet, if it were
really 'no big deal,' then what was she doing in Dr
Pipher's office to begin with? Answer: she was threatening to kill herself.[5]

The reason for the devastation, of course, is because of the
sense of rejection that inevitably follows upon broken and
transitory sexual relationships. One gives one's all, reveals
one's deepest self, to somebody – only for the relationship to
be over in a short time. And the only defence against this vul-
nerability, of course, is not to care too much in the first place,
to treat sex as a plaything, and one's body as just another
form of recreation. But when millions and millions of us do
this, it simply reinforces our sense of isolation and of unlov-
ableness. If we cannot – or do not dare – love deeply
and unreservedly, why should anybody love us deeply and
unreservedly?

The 'liberation' of sex from the constraints of traditional
morality has, then, been a re-run of the 'liberation' of
humanity from God: at the very moment of being absolu-
tized, it has thereby been trivialized and rendered worthless.
Having been desacralized, it becomes a mere object like any
other. Instead of being a guarantor of our specialness, we
are once more left alone.

Yet, once we have embraced the culture of promiscuity, it
becomes a fetish that we simply will not let go. How could
we? After so thoroughly defiling our own lives, what else
would we have? It is the defence of the freedom to be
promiscuous that accounts for the passion with which abortion rights are defended, and for the insistent batting away
and studious ignoring of the mounting evidence of harm
which the sexualized culture does to our lives. Consider the
irrational audience responses at a recent radio discussion
programme:

DONNA HERFORD: What are your thoughts on
enabling unmarried couples to adopt?

TIM COLLINS (Shadow Minister to the Cabinet
Office): Let me preface what I'm about to say by
saying that there are very many deeply loving and
deeply successful cohabiting and indeed same-sex
couples in this country who are already bringing up
children and there are people of goodwill on both
sides of this issue in all the political parties.

My view, however, is that we should start from the
viewpoint of the interests of the children . . .

If a child is brought up by parents who are not
married it is twice as likely to suffer from mental
illness as . . . if it's brought up by parents who are
married, three times more likely to run away from
home and – this is the real shocker – 33 times more
likely to suffer serious abuse . . .

What those children most desperately need is
stability and again here, I'm afraid, I don't think we
can ignore the statistics.

[Over a period of] five years only eight per cent of
. . . married couples will have broken up . . . but 52
per cent of cohabiting couples will have broken up
after five years . . .

NICOLA STURGEON (Health and Community Care
spokeswoman for the Scottish National Party): It
seems to me entirely contradictory to say on the one
hand all that matters is the interest of the child and
on the other hand to try and impose your own view
of what the family unit should look like, regardless
of the interests of the child.

[CLAPPING]

You know there are a lot . . . of children out there
who are living with Mum and Dad and they'll be
miserable because their parents' relationships are
miserable, and in my view all that matters is that an

individual or a couple, whether heterosexual, married, unmarried or indeed gay, can offer a child a safe, secure, and loving home life and environment, and if that's the case then surely that's what's in the interest of the child.

And we live in a society where children are living in all sorts of circumstances, and perhaps we should get away from trying to convince everybody that the only valid and legitimate family unit is 2.4 kids and Mum and Dad because what that does is devalue and de-legitimize the living circumstances of many other children who don't live in those circumstances.
[CLAPPING][6]

Never mind the facts or the statistics that indicate what *will* happen; they are met with stony silence. Upholding a moral framework as normative may 'devalue' or 'de-legitimize' those who live outside of it. Ms Sturgeon was right about one thing: to uphold a value is to stigmatize its opposite. That is what all traditional societies have accepted in respect of morality. But, as the applause showed, it is a price that we flatly refuse to pay.

By upholding amorality as a value (or rather, an anti-value), however, we thereby stigmatize *its* opposite: think, for example, of the sneering discussions of sexual decency (constant innuendo of sexual inadequacy or suppressed disorders) and the previously noticed condescension towards religion in our public discourse. Consider the use of 'judgementalism' (a term itself implying a negative judgement on the person or opinion concerned) to stigmatize the making of any traditional moral judgements, however meekly expressed.

Yet we can hardly argue that the sexual revolution has done us no harm. Shalit points to instance after instance of young women like Kelli in her example above who have come to loathe themselves. She argues that all manner of modern psychological conditions among young people –

especially young women – have their roots in sexual rejection or having been abused, or simply in attempts to keep others at a distance (and, as in the case of anorexia, to reduce one's feminine sex appeal and 'stay in control'). Certainly this corresponds very closely indeed with my own pastoral experience.

'Why', she asks, 'are none of my grandmother's friends anorexic? Why are even the plumpest of them contented?'[7] Lest this be thought facile (most grandmothers, after all, are beyond worrying about their sex appeal or trying to keep men at a distance), the point is that they never were anorexic (or bulimic or self-harming). The problem is ours. We have created the 'problem' of 'self-esteem'. Few of the grandma generation experienced the kind of rejection that is now the lot of almost all teenage girls from their early sexual experiences.

In this aspect of life as in others, traditional morality lends dignity to those who know they are under an obligation to uphold it. It is this that non-Westerners can still see but which we cannot.

> One of modesty's paradoxes . . . is that it is usually a reflection of self-worth, of having such a high opinion of yourself that you don't need to boast or put your body on display for all to see. A modestly dressed woman is one who is too important for 'public use'. On the other hand, it is bragging and exhibitionism which we instinctively associate with insecurity . . . In this light, it makes sense that so many studies should find early sexual intercourse for girls to be correlated with low self-esteem . . .[8]

Neither are adolescence and early adulthood the beginning and end of our problems in this area. The purely emotional function to which families have been reduced has greatly increased the expectation among middle-aged adults to remain 'sexy' – if only to boost their own self-esteem. The possibility of reinventing their lives – along with the heightened risk that they may be forced to do so if their spouse deserts them – means that they would be ill-advised to rule out even the theoretical possibility of further amours.

The fragility of families; the extension of adolescent social expectations (partying, nights out with 'the boys'/'the girls') into adult life; the pervasiveness of the sexualized culture created by the media; the contingent nature of our self-image in a whirling social melting-pot – all these things mean that it is almost impossible not to 'buy in' to the sexualized culture, at least to some extent.

## *The adolescent crisis*

If adolescents have, in material terms, an absolute paradise in the contemporary West, they nevertheless experience a very hard time, emotionally speaking. Traditional societies taught their young early to know who and what they were. To perpetuate the community's faith and practices was a sacred duty; to inherit the family's land (or trade or business) was an elementary expectation; at a minimum, to prove oneself to be 'one's father's son' or 'one's mother's daughter' was a matter of pride. Such knowledge and expectation were supported by both peer pressure and daily example and so were strong enough to survive the accidental misfortunes (an invasion, a bankruptcy, a disreputable parent) that might have served to call this way of thinking into question or shatter a person's sense of identity.

This is not to say that everyone was blissfully happy, of course! Such a world was very limited and limiting. Its disadvantages were different from those of our world. Yet it is this stability that Western modernity has destroyed. Starting with the Industrial Revolution, rootedness to place was replaced by getting on one's bike to find work. The suffocating familiarity of the village was replaced by the disorientating anonymity of the city. If Marx could speak of 'the idiocy of rural life', then the person rooted to place was the idiot, who was now derided for an ignorant bumpkin; he has made way for the commuter, the tourist and, in our own day, for the knowing cosmopolitan. In traditional society, the loner was to be feared (witches, you remember, always lived in the forest, didn't they?); in modernity, as in the Wild West, the Lone Ranger was the hero. In sixteenth- and seventeenth-century England, 'innovation' was a label one attempted to fasten round the neck of one's political or religious enemy in order to prove he was wrong; in Blair-speak, 'conservatism' (even with a small 'c') is a swear word. Pre-moderns knew who they were – and who other people were – by reference to their families. In modern society, the teenager must prove himself an adult by 'finding himself' and 'becoming his own person', and he is to do this precisely by rejecting his family: the crisis of adolescence is a crisis of our own making (in more than one sense of that phrase).

Traditional restrictions are to be cast aside so that the individual can assert his or her own independence and define his or her own selfhood. This has been elevated to the supreme Western value, which the shift to post-modernity has not reversed, but reinforced. Yet the modernist affirmation of selfhood generally brought ambiguous gains, and made 'the self' problematic. Arranged marriages were out – men and women themselves should choose their spouse for love, not have one imposed by 'parents who know best' (or who may have wider agendas of their own). The result has been marriages that depend on emotion, rather than being rooted in wider social and economic needs, and are thus far more fragile and prone to divorce (another innovation of personal choice) than what they have replaced: 'an American marries the woman he loves, but an Indian loves the woman he marries'. David Steel and his fellow campaigners in the 1960s promised that legalized abortion would make 'every child a wanted child', that is, a result of personal choice and self-affirmation rather than an imposition of nature. By the end of the twentieth century, the supposed gains in the 'wantedness' of children were not exactly obvious, at least not by reference to all of the indicators of child abuse or child neglect. And the adolescent, having once 'invented' himself or herself in distinction from parents and family, now mostly finds that the process can be, or has to be, repeated throughout life, as he or she moves from one job or career, one geographical location or sexual partner, one group of friends, one religious or philosophical 'commitment', to another – and then to another. Indeed, the very idea of 'commitment', superficially so conservative, in fact exalts the self as chooser of relationships, systems of morals, beliefs and so on, rather than as the recipient of, and participant in, these things as 'given'. It is thereby a term that affirms self-invention, and thus the contingency of identity upon (mutable) personal choices.[9]

Modernity elevated the 'essence' of the self, hoping to free it from the shackles of its social location, that is, imposed identity. The Rousseauian vision of the heroic self that needed to be recovered from the poisoned atmosphere of actual social conditions fuelled the revolutions of the nineteenth and twentieth centuries, which all claimed to be for 'liberty', whether defined in nationalist or socialist terms. Once achieved, the revolutions (particularly of the latter type) appeared to submerge the individual in the mass; the thrill was not in their attainment, but in the striving after them, and the postures of moral righteousness they enabled their protagonists to obtain in railing against the limitations that the *anciens régimes* placed in the way of self-fulfilment.

All of the modernist projects, whether capitalist, nationalist or socialist, dissolved traditional categories of identity. To be sure, nationalism and socialism erected new categories (those of nationhood and of class) to replace the old, but these were abstractions that had been self-consciously

constructed for the purposes of furthering present antagon-
isms; they could not reassure and console in the way that
the old verities of family, ancestors, village, and inherited
personal loyalties could. Orthodoxy in medieval Russia
contributed to conferring identity on peasants because of its
immediacy and the tangibility of its rituals, *not* because it
was 'the soul of Russian-ness'. The latter construct is a
large-scale abstract, useful for encouraging fascistic tendencies in the modern era, perhaps, but less stable in conveying
identity. Capitalism did not even provide new categories
to replace the old. The self was alone; its ideal was the
'self-made man'.

All of this was sustainable while enough of stable social
conditions remained intact for the content and meaning of
the 'essential self' to be somehow above the need for inves-
tigation, a topic about which most people could remain
unreflective. But once the social demolition of imposed identities had become all too successful, a point generally
reached in Western societies since the Second World War,
the rootlessness of individuals left adrift in an anonymous
pea-soup of humanity has become apparent. At that point,
the question 'Who am I?' becomes more than a matter for
philosophically minded souls, who have toyed with it down
the ages; it becomes an issue for every person. 'My identity'
becomes a big issue – especially for the adolescent.

The problem of rootlessness has been compounded by
the post-modern ideology (a contradiction in terms, of
course – but then, post-modernity is big on irony) of repudiating all distinctions between people, or at least of making
them newly problematic. Nowhere is this more true than in
respect of sex and identity. Anyone who is too sure of his or
her identity (and, by necessary implication, of the identity of
others) in this area is laying themselves wide open to denun-
ciation. In consequence, few now are sure of what it means
to 'be a man' or 'be a woman'; a basic aspect of existence
has been rendered problematic. The attack on traditional

roles and the assault on 'stereotypes' were doubtless intended to set free groups deemed to have been oppressed by past metanarratives. But by kicking them aside, we render our own situatedness and identities problematic, since we only know who we are in relation to others. By forbidding ourselves to discriminate, we forbid ourselves to discern.

By having no settled culture, no fixed identity to which a person is expected to conform – that is, by expecting each person to make his or her own way in the world and invent his or her own life – the phenomenon of the adolescent identity crisis has been created.

And this crisis is a marketing bonanza. By playing on it and accentuating it, all manner of goods may be sold. When people are constantly told an updated version of 'clothes maketh the man' (that is, that the latest consumer artefacts are the path to self-actualization), it is no wonder that advertising is kicking on an open door when it tries to capitalize on the new insecurities of youth (new, at least, since the 1950s) in order to sell products. Older adults are too quick to condemn, for actually this insanity makes perfectly good sense in its context. When there are no norms to which I must conform, no family or tradition which can tell me who I am, no belief-system which cannot be debunked (by me or, failing that, by the teachers, entertainers and other spokesmen and spokeswomen for the society around me) on the basis of commonplace rationalism, then I am adrift. I am 'condemned to be free', for 'every man, without any support or help whatever, is condemned at every instant to invent man'.[10] Who is to say that obtaining the latest pair of trainers will not be my salvation? For the moment, at least, it may be exactly that – and what identity, in the post-modern world, lasts longer than 'the moment'?

At that point, consumerist artefacts, fashion and entertainment assume grotesque levels of importance. The first two are the vehicles for creating our ephemeral identities –

and therefore to be without something that our peers (or those whose peers we aspire to be) deem desirable is to suffer a loss of selfhood. The last, entertainment, gives us a fund of stories with which to invest our lives with the illusion of meaning, and of characters whose mannerisms and behaviour we can ape, in the hope that this might make us 'somebody'.

Little wonder that a desire for fame for its own sake becomes all-consuming for many young people. The content of the fame (it might even be notoriety) is almost immaterial. Its importance lies in the fact that it is a rescue from the intolerable oppression of anonymity. The vacuous TV celebrity is famous, as often as not, merely for being famous. And yet the imaginations of millions are fired by little else. More than one commentator has noticed that the tawdry domestic dramas played out in the lives of many of the poorest are almost a conscious imitation of the soap operas on television. Life imitates art – if soap operas count as art. This situation has a certain logic about it. In the absence of a guaranteed place in society, through the recognition of family, or automatic respect for our maleness or femaleness, only fame (that is, the recognition of others) can assure us that we are fully real, that we count. And, in the absence of that, the emulation of the famous will have to serve.

As our Western world intrudes ever more upon non-Western space, we believe ourselves to be offering freedoms, prosperity and rising aspirations. And, in a sense, we are. But we are also seen as deracinated egotists, rooted in no solid culture and no fixed network of family and relationships. The things that we believe ourselves to be promoting do indeed appeal to non-Westerners. But, quite understandably, not all of them are ready to throw themselves into the moral and social void in the process. Understandably, they wish to know if the Western trinkets can be bought at a lower price.

## Humility and self-worth – or arrogance and self-loathing?

Compare the current Western *angst*-ridden environment with the assumptions of the age of Isaac Watts (1674–1748). As with the great hymn writer, so with all of us: it is what we say subconsciously, or by the way, that is often most revealing of our true state of mind. Consider the first and last verses of his most famous hymn:

> When I survey the wondrous cross
> On which the Prince of Glory died,
> My richest gain I count but loss
> And pour contempt on all my pride.
>
> Were the whole realm of nature mine,
> That were an off'ring far too small;
> Love so amazing, so divine,
> Demands my soul, my life, my all.

The central message of the hymn is obvious: the sacrifice of Christ on the cross and the magnitude of his love shown by that redemption inspire us to give ourselves to him and to his service. In the process we are to abase ourselves and 'pour contempt on all [our] pride', boasting in nothing but 'the death of Christ, [our] God'. Yet this self-abasement and recognition of our own sinfulness are nevertheless a million miles removed from modern Western self-loathing. On the contrary, they are compatible with an innate certainty of self-worth that, sadly, eludes us. It is the last verse of the hymn that reveals the true assumption about the evaluation of the self, precisely because of the off-handedness of the way in which it is mentioned. 'The whole realm of nature' is an inadequate gift to devote by way of thanks for God's grace; only 'my soul, my life, my all' will do. What kind of megalomaniac, some might ask, thinks that his or her own person is worth more, in the sight of God, than 'the whole realm of nature'? Certainly our culture has no such confidence. And yet the words have been sung with assurance by countless thousands who had no vote, little or no control over their lives, and could be – indeed, were – ordered around every day of their lives by others who, through mere accident of birth, were their social superiors! Did they suffer from a 'crisis of self-esteem'? Apparently not!

And that raises the question: *why* not? How did people who lived in material and political conditions that would strike us as degrading (and bear an uncanny resemblance to the conditions in which five-sixths of humanity still lives) nevertheless take it for granted that 'my soul, my life, my all' is of enormous worth?

There are two possible answers. On the one hand, it could be argued that the answer lies in the nature of the Christian faith itself, which assures people that, though they are sinful, the infinite–personal God of the universe loves them – indeed, that he loves them so much that he sent his Son to die for their sins. On the other hand, it could be argued that the answer lies in the nature of traditional society itself, which roots most people in a family, guarantees them a place (even a lowly place) and invests their lives with meaning. Even those people who had suffered uncommon disasters in these areas knew by daily observation that their lot was atypical, that they could still 'fit in', that they were not ineluctably cast adrift in the world.

I would suggest that both answers have a degree of explanatory power. And, far from accidentally, the postmodern West has rejected both Christianity and the world of social stability. Our daily experience tells us, instead, that we are 'free', that we are masters of our fate with no guidelines from a tyrannous god nor from a patriarchal tradition – that is, that we are inevitably alone, in a world without purpose, meaning or stability. We scream out for 'relationships' precisely because, for us, they are problematic and highly contingent. Even those who are blessed with uncommon stability and happiness know by daily observation that their lot is atypical – that they are liable to be cast adrift at any time. As Wendy Shalit observes,

> What's rarely talked about is what it's like to grow up in a divorce culture even when your parents are not divorced. For even when they're happy, they always could get divorced . . . My generation has grown up living in the constant awareness that we cannot depend on anyone but ourselves . . . We are constantly judged and reevaluated, even by our lovers, the ones with whom it was once thought one could rest.[11]

In consequence, though we make a cult of 'self-esteem' and 'assertiveness', though we angrily reject the idea of our sinfulness and its concomitant, personal obligations; though we think self-abasement (or even ordinary humility) to be a form of sickness, we nevertheless despise ourselves. What would the impoverished inhabitants of early eighteenth-century England have made of us? Truly, we have gained the world, and lost our own souls.

# Observations in passing? The demographic trump card

In January 2003, BBC radio broadcast a current affairs programme about a baby-boom in France. Birth rates in that
country have been rising for a few years, aided, it was
alleged, by certain of its government's policies. Children's
playground chatter hummed happily away in the background to the announcer's voice. Surely, the impression was
given, France's population is set to rise.

But despite the programme's upbeat note, the truth
leaked out in one casually mentioned statistic – though its
meaning was not explained, nor were its consequences
made clear. The birth rate in France has now risen to 1.9
children per woman. Given that, for a population to replace
itself, the rate needs to be 2.1, this means merely that the
French population is dying out a little more slowly than that
of other Western countries. Why, at this rate, it will take a
whole seven generations for it to fall to half its present level!
The rest of us should be so lucky; we are dying out much
more quickly.

Of course, it should be pointed out that the birth rate will
not be identical across the French population as a whole.
Certain groups within society will be declining more rapidly
than the overall statistic implies; others will actually be
increasing. In the latter camp will be France's large number
of Muslim immigrants (mostly from north Africa) and their

descendants. There are enough of them now to affect the national average of 1.9 children per woman; without them, the figure would have been lower. The true picture that emerges, then, is one of gradual decline of the population at large, with a more rapid shrinkage among the indigenous – and especially the middle-class – elements and a rise, perhaps quite sharp, among the newcomers.

Even this scenario fails to allow for future immigration, which will certainly be very significant in the years ahead. The true picture may be one in which, sometime late this century, the descendants of the present indigenous French are barely a majority in France.

The erosion elsewhere in the West is much more far-reaching, and consequently the resultant social volatility will occur much sooner. If we have witnessed the first stirrings of quasi-fascistic movements across Europe in the past few years, one shudders to think what lies ahead of us. Of course, racism and fascism will be no more justified in the 2030s and 2040s than they are now, and for two reasons. In the first place, the blame for the very natural sense of deep unease that is – and will continue to be – felt by the indigenous Western populations lies, not with the newcomers, but with the Westerners themselves. For it is their culture that has failed the first and most vital test of any human culture: it cannot reproduce itself into the future. In the second place, many of the immigrants come from cultures that can, and that ability is rooted in a closer adherence to traditional morality.

For if there's one thing that is quite certain about the sexual revolution of the 1960s, it is that it isn't sexy. The westernized populations of the earth that have adopted it are not, for the most part, having babies. The problem afflicts North America, Australasia and Japan. It affects all of Europe with the exception of just one country: Muslim Albania. As we shall see, the reality is a little more complex – and, on closer inspection, even more worrying – than this simple fact might suggest, but it remains the salient fact that we need to take into account in understanding the dynamic of what is happening.

I have argued throughout that Western culture since the Enlightenment has diverged further and further from the common values of all previously existing societies. Much of this change has been related to the Industrial Revolution and its inevitable consequences for our manner of life. Since this process both accompanied and facilitated rising living standards and increasing freedoms, it might fairly be judged that many of the changes constituted an actual improvement on the common features of pre-modern societies. In particular, the move towards an impersonal state and impersonal models of authority greatly facilitated efficiency and personal freedoms. The backwash of the Reformation cult of 'integrity' had an even better effect, greatly enhancing the advance of commerce and making political freedoms compatible with continuing good social order.

But the ease with which Westerners came to dominate the globe during the eighteenth and nineteenth centuries has allowed them to slip into a fatal complacency about their rejection of the human past and has caused the culture of renunciation to become ever more exaggerated. During the twentieth century, what I have called the 'qualities of barbarism' have become more pronounced as the modernization process has moved into overdrive and prosperity has become hyper-prosperity. In consequence, our lives have become ever more detached from the fundamental realities of human existence and ever more enclosed within consumerist, piped-entertainment cocoons.

As the sexual freedoms that the past two generations of Westerners have granted themselves have become a central feature of their social lives, their entertainment and even of their legislation, so they have collided with the most fundamental reality of all. They are not reproducing themselves.

Non-Westerners, meanwhile, could not be so detached. As the Western anti-values have impinged ever more on their lives and begun to undermine their own cultures, so their relative impotence vis-à-vis Westerners has become ever more irksome to them. In recent years, however, non-Westerners have discovered the means of challenging Western domination at the very moment when many of them are themselves embarking upon the processes of modernization, economic growth and urbanization. This presents them with a dilemma: they feel the pressure within their own societies to embark on the same trajectory of cultural deracination that Western societies have followed, while at the same time their new-found economic strength is creating a groundswell of renewed cultural self-confidence that is pushing them in the opposite direction.

## Growing old disgracefully

Unfortunately, Western population decline coincides with medical and other advances that mean that we are all living longer. This makes it possible to obfuscate about this issue by pretending that the looming pensions crisis and the growing imbalance between the working age population and the retired populations – a crisis that is only just beginning and will not come to a climax until the second decade of the century – are simply an unfortunate consequence of rising living standards and better health.

In fact, however, the working-age population is set to fall, not just relative to the mushrooming numbers of old people, but absolutely. In other words the crisis is a result not just of increasing longevity, but also of decreasing fertility. What is worse, once this process begins, it accentuates itself. If working people need to carry the burden (let us abandon all euphemisms and talk straight economics here!) of a large retired population, the financial squeeze they experience will cause them to delay child-bearing until even later, or to have fewer children at all. (In terms of demographic consequences, the former choice is only a milder version of the latter.)

No amount of fiddling with pension and health systems can avoid the consequences of this elephantine fact. Public-sector or private schemes; pay-as-you-go or insurance principle; interest rates and dividends or income from property rental: none can do more than optimize the unavoidable circumstance that retired people live off the economy that is kept running by the workers. That being so, the ratio of workers to retired people is of profound significance for the welfare of both groups. Our propensity to keep tinkering with the mechanisms is a measure of how far the comfort of Westerners' lives has caused them to lose contact with fundamental realities: surely there must be a technocratic solution! Surely a hike in interest rates here, a tax incentive there, a re-allocation of resources along such-and-such lines will resolve the issue. Surely this moral problem can be side-stepped by a technical fix; the problem, after all, as Helvétius would have told us, 'is not the wickedness of men, but the ignorance of lawmakers'. But is it? Is it?

Neither statist nor free-trade dogmas – that is, neither public nor private sector solutions – make any difference; both of them have long since been used to 'socialize' the costs of pensions and provision for the elderly. As individuals, we come to think that we do not need children to provide for our old age, for it will be paid for by a 'them', whether government pension or private savings scheme. That is, we can live off the labours of other people's children. Let us only hope that not too many of the others think the same way.

Increased longevity actually increases the degree of dependence of the old on the young compared with what was experienced by previous societies (and in the Third World, still is experienced), even when we have made all allowances for the fact that we can now also remain fitter for longer. When Bismarck introduced retirement at the age of 65, average life expectancy in Germany was just 45. He could rely on the fact that only a small minority would ever qualify for the state help that he proffered them. When the same measure was introduced in the UK in the early twentieth century, the average age at death was just 48. Now, almost all of us survive into our (usually quite prolonged) dotages. And this, up to a point, is all to the good. But it means that in old age we are more – not less – dependent on the young than our ancestors were. There are more of us to support, and we will need supporting for much longer.

## *Baby hunger and its causes*

The socialization of provision for age, however, makes the individual more careless of this fact. Because of it, Westerners have lost one of the primeval urges to reproduce. To be sure, our genes continue to drive the instinctive sex urge; that is one of nature's (or, as we used to say, God's) ways of persuading us to 'be fruitful and multiply'. But, except for a few short periods in our lives when we may actually be wanting 'to go for a baby', pregnancy is now considered to be an occupational hazard of sexual activity, rather than something intrinsically bound up with it. In the twentieth century, Westerners found very effective ways to separate the satisfaction of the sexual urge from its naturally or divinely intended consequence.

In our own minds, we have made the separation in order to be 'liberated' from oppressive moral strictures, and to maximize our opportunities for sexual enjoyment without embarrassing ourselves by tell-tale pregnancies. Even if the enjoyment is only with our legal and above-board spouse, however, we nevertheless wish not to burden our finances and careers with more children than our aspirations for Greek holidays can stand.

To be sure, our opportunities for sexual enjoyment have indeed mushroomed in the past 70 years or so, though whether we are actually happier in this area is highly questionable; every single survey shows that married women, for example, are more sexually fulfilled than their unmarried but sexually active counterparts. One can understand the reticence of the latter to tie the knot; in a society where promiscuity is rife, most women have a huge difficulty in finding a man who can be relied on – and they are understandably 'placing their bets' as late as possible. So they are marrying later, if at all – a choice that is itself full of consequence for future demography. Furthermore, to attain this chimerical sexual nirvana, we have succeeded all too well in curtailing the very fertility towards which the sexual urge is directed in the first place. In consequence, birth rates have plunged in every single society that has abandoned traditional sexual morality – which includes, for this purpose, the former communist countries of eastern Europe.

Why are Western populations unable to replace themselves? Let us consider first and foremost the quantifiable factors. Abortion ends the lives of millions of children every year. Without the abortion law of 1973, the US population would today have 40 million more young people than it does at present (or, in fact, more – for they would certainly, by now, have had many children on their own account). As early as 1983, 30 per cent of all pregnancies in the USA were terminated by abortion. Can we seriously imagine that such a circumstance could have had anything other than the gravest effect upon our demography? The UK has lost six million potential citizens since 1967, by the same method.

Other factors also play a role. The massive prolongation of education has raised the age at which most people wish to marry or have children. The late age of marriage caused by emphasis on careers (and the above-mentioned difficulty that women have in finding a reliable man) means that married couples have fewer children. Double-earning couples delay childbirth further. The pursuit of the 'good life' means that few couples wish to have more than one or two children. And more and more of us are consciously choosing not to have children at all.

We might argue with some justice that all of these things are perfectly legitimate and justifiable choices. But the consequences for our demography indicate otherwise. It is no accident that all pre-modern societies considered that a person's first social duty was to marry and have children – a duty reflected in all religious codes. The personal misfortune of childlessness or the religious vocation to the priesthood or the cloister apart, this was the normative pattern. We, of course, have full liberty to think otherwise, and to reject this conception of duty, along with all other duties, but nature has the liberty – and the observable habit – of 'snapping back' on us, because we violate the kind of place that the world is, and has been created to be.

At the margins, other features unique to (or rather, particularly pronounced in) Western societies chip away at the edges of demographic patterns, each of them dragging the graph downwards just a little more. The numbers of people who are unwillingly childless is growing. Anorexia, an illness more or less peculiar to the modern West, leaves some of its erstwhile sufferers unable to conceive. Sexual abuse of children sometimes, horrifically, has the same effect – and such abuse is on the increase. (Children living in homes where their mothers have serial boyfriends are over 30 times more likely to be abused than those living with their married parents. Since the former category is rising and the latter declining, levels of abuse will continue to rise also.) Abortions can have the same effect, much though 'pro-choice' protagonists try to stifle discussion of the matter.

Pre-modern societies, of course, did not make many allowances for homosexuality; all people were expected to marry. Indeed, Plato makes explicit reference to the fact that many men married and had children out of a sense of social duty – and then found friendship and recreation in other ways.[1] Many will find it laudable that few people feel such social pressures today – but that freedom, too, gets fed into the statistics.

Many of the factors that have been surveyed in this book have jointly conduced to bring about demographic decline: the sexualization of society; the desire to maintain the 'freedom' of an adolescent lifestyle for as long as possible, including after marriage; addiction to short-term consumerist hyper-prosperity and the (false) assumption that the demographic future and our own old age will take care of themselves; the loss of any sense of being custodians of a human tradition that we are obliged to pass on to the future; the aggressive self-assertion fostered by the 'rights culture' which we use to vilify restraint and obligations and to legitimize even the most petulant of our immediate desires; the division between private and public worlds whereby we have come to believe that sexual behaviour (that is, the essential mechanism by which a society perpetuates itself into the future) is a matter entirely for personal choice; the possibility, via the bourgeoisification of Western societies, of work becoming a means of self-actualization – rather than of family support.

Our global domination and stratospheric living standards have confirmed us in an unfounded confidence in the rightness of these attitudes. They have also deluded us into an over-haughty rejection of the wisdom of the ages which was enshrined in societies all around us. 'Just look at the mess they are in!' we have cried. 'What do we have to learn from them?' (And we all too easily overlooked the fact that part, at least, of that mess was the fault of Western colonization – and then decolonization – producing long-term political crises of legitimacy in the non-West, crises that were then exacerbated by the relentless export of the Western anti-culture.)

Even as early as the mid-1970s, the front cover of the West German magazine *Der Spiegel* was asking anxiously '*Sterben die Deutschen aus?*' ('Are the Germans dying out?') By the end of the twentieth century the answer was clear enough: Germany had a birth rate of just 1.4 children per woman – only two-thirds of replacement rate. No wonder Germany was the first country to find that pensions had become a hot political issue. At that rate, in the absence of immigration, Germany's population would fall from 82 million now to 38.5 million in 2100. Of course, a drop of that magnitude in the levels of occupation of such a rich country will not happen in reality. For it would create a social, political and demographic vacuum that simply could not – and would not – be left unfilled. No, the only two realistic possibilities for Germany in the twenty-first century are a vast increase in immigration or an unimaginable increase in the German birth rate. And, here, I no longer need to argue a case: which of these two outcomes, in the judgement of any observant person, is the likelier?

The UK is doing only a little better, with a rate of just 1.69 children per woman. That gives its present population level of 60 million a half-life (given hypothetical zero immigration) of almost 150 years. But the combination of an ageing population with a massive cultural shift under the demographic impact of newcomers and their descendants can safely be predicted to make for lively politics by the 2030s or 2040s at the very latest.

Feminism and the sexual revolution came relatively late to Roman Catholic parts of Europe, but when they did arrive they came with a vengeance. Birth rates in Italy and Spain are now at catastrophic levels: 1.19 and 1.07 respectively. Italy will need to absorb five million immigrants a decade just to keep its population level steady. A United Nations report in 2002 estimated that the EU would need to import 1.58 million immigrants annually between now and 2050 (that is, a total of 75 million people over the whole period) to keep its working population at present levels. If it wishes to keep the existing ratio of workers to retired people, it will need far, far more. As Peter Drucker observes, 'the most important single new certainty . . . is the collapsing birthrate in the developed world.'[2] Normally, the median age for a healthy society is in the high 20s and low 30s. But Japan, the oldest society in the world today, now has a median age of 40. That is set to be far exceeded by southern Europeans in the middle of this century; in the absence of massive immigration, the figure will be close to the mid-50s.

Perhaps the most depressing thing, in the face of this meltdown, is the refusal of many of those who are prepared to admit to the fact of it to take it all seriously. Paul Wallace's book *Agequake* is a guide to companies, investors and property managers as to how to make money out of the demographic 'rollercoaster' (as he cheerily calls it) that lies ahead of us. His chapters and sections have headings such as 'Modern Methuselahs', 'The new property game' and 'The new business game'. Every time his bright and breezy style comes close to fingering a real social dilemma, he tiptoes swiftly back from the brink of 'moralizing' and returns to the safer ground of avoiding stock losses.[3]

Perhaps I am being too harsh. We shall all benefit from the likes of Wallace and those who take his advice, for the simple reason that market forces and the price mechanism act, in the long run, as a reality-check for individuals and even, eventually, for governments. They do this by forcing us to turn away from pontificating about where certain courses of action *ought* to lead, and to pay attention instead to where, in all rational calculation, they *will* lead. And market forces will compel us to confront the consequences of disintegrating families and population decline long before the theoretical meltdown is reached.

For, on a zero-immigration hypothesis, the European population as a whole (including that of the former Soviet Union) is set to fall from 728 million today to 207 million by 2100 – that is, to 28.4 per cent of its present level. As the right-wing American commentator Pat Buchanan observes, 'This is not a matter of prophecy, but of mathematics.'[4] And yet, obviously, it remains a merely mathematical construct.

A population collapse of this magnitude will not happen in reality, for sharp fiscal and economic constraints, or even other kinds of social, political and economic collapse, would kick in long before that point was reached – which raises the question: what will happen instead?

## Better than average: the indigenous underclass and immigrants

Up to this point, we have been dealing only in hard fact. Those who are uncomfortable with the direction in which our analysis points leave themselves wide open to the rejoinder 'Never mind value judgements: which part of the mathematics do you disagree with?' But I wish to stress that what follows is more speculative in nature, for it deals with non-quantifiable elements of the future. Nevertheless, I have sought to establish it as firmly on the basis of the mathematically knowable as I can – even if it remains speculation.

Some of the considerations mentioned above that combine to drive birth rates downwards – 'careers', late marriage, pursuit of the material 'good life' – all apply far more strongly to the Western middle classes than to the underclass. The terrifying average birth rates of Western societies are the result of even more catastrophic averages among the middle classes, which are then modified by higher rates (replacement or better) among other groups.

The indigenous poor, those who are unemployed or have marginal jobs, those whose schooling left them with little in the way of skills and qualifications: these elements in Western societies do not fit so easily into the patterns of behaviour described above. If young women from these groups fail to marry it is not, in general, because they wish to pursue their education followed by a geographically mobile career. Neither do they consider their singleness a signal, to themselves and others, that they are not yet ready to have children. On the contrary: childbirth often comes earlier and more frequently than it does to their middle-class peers. Many have demographically 'replaced themselves' by their early 20s, without ever bothering about ties of marriage at all. And as for finding a reliable man with whom to have children, Geoffrey Dench has pointed out that this has become a virtual impossibility among the uneducated and underemployed.[5] Instead, having children is not a commitment to a partner so much as a consolation to the mother for being forced to live in a criminalized and brutalized environment; not a financial burden to be embraced with trepidation so much as a career move and a guarantee of being given public housing.[6]

This phenomenon can be seen, albeit with some distorting elements, in two statistics. Approximately 35 per cent of children in the UK are now born out of wedlock. This figure has vacillated, over the centuries, between 2 per cent and 6 per cent, kept down by strong public disapproval. That disapproval has now evaporated; only the quasi-assurance provided to women by the much weakened bond of marriage prevents the illegitimacy rate from rising even higher. But it is overwhelmingly middle-class women, whose material and social expectations give them something to lose, who are at all insistent upon such reassurances. The weaker that marriage bonds become, the more illegitimacy rates will continue to rise and overall birth rates will continue to fall.

The other statistic is the 25 per cent of British children living in homes where there is no full-time breadwinner. What makes this statistic so eye-catching is the fact that the unemployment rate is much, much lower than this; even allowing for differences in interpretation of the official figures, it is not above 5 per cent. Are adults living with children really five times more likely to be unemployed than their childless counterparts? Even allowing for large numbers of divorced and separated wives, it is hard not to conclude that the single mothers of the underclass are producing, not simply at younger ages, but more often, than the population as a whole. The under-employed and under-educated are helping to boost the population. With the passing of the years, they inevitably come to constitute a larger share of it.

The other segment of the population that is helping to hold up birth rates is achieving the feat for very different reasons – indeed, for exactly opposite reasons. Some kinds of non-Western immigrants, but by no means all, have held on to the importance of marriage, family and chastity. In so doing, they make the host populations look down on them as 'backward' or 'outdated'. But for these very reasons, their birth rates are higher. Mostly, they come from strong ancient cultures whose values remind us – or should remind us – that marriage and the family are about preventing us from having to choose between fecundity and order. The indigenous Westerners themselves have abandoned solid family structures and 'liberalized' their sexual behaviour. In doing so, they have divided into two broad patterns: the middle class, who maintain social order (because they have a high vested interest in it, in the form of property, career aspirations and so on) but do not reproduce; and the under-class, who do reproduce, but are increasingly criminalized, ghettoized and under-educated. (Dr Theodore Dalrymple observes that a huge proportion of domestic violence visited on his inner-city patients is rooted in sexual jealousy and lack of trust: 'if people demand sexual liberty for them-selves, but sexual fidelity from others, the result is the inflammation of jealousy . . . [which] is the most frequent precipitant of violence between the sexes.' In the catchment area of his hospital, one in five women between the ages of 16 and 50 attends the emergency department each year, suf-fering from injuries sustained in this manner.[7]) Domestic violence against women affects some of the non-Western immigrants too, of course. Nevertheless, those groups that keep their family structures, religious observances and tra-ditional morality will be saved – in the long run and on the law of statistical averages – from having to make the choice between fecundity and social order. By maintaining sexual morality, they can have both.

Other immigrant groups, however, approximate much more nearly to the patterns already obtaining in Western countries, usually because they assimilate quickly. In doing so, their own birth rates fall.

And this is the irony of the immigrant phenomenon. Only massive immigration during the years ahead can fend off the West's demographic decline, prevent the collapse of our pension and health-care systems upon which our ageing populations depend, and keep the working-age population – and so the economy – from coming under an intolerable tax burden. Yet if those immigrants assimilate to the secular social patterns of their host countries, they do not help to resolve the West's problem – or at least, they do so only for one generation. They merely serve to delay the demographic collapse for their own lifetimes, rather than help to internalize an 'upward push'.

To prevent demographic decline in the long term, only *non*-assimilating migrants will do! Those who come from strong traditional cultures, and maintain them even after moving to the West, will 'replace themselves' (or better) demographically, and so help to even out the decline among the indigenous middle classes. Those who become westernized, on the other hand, will adopt Western behaviour patterns and have fewer children as a result. That is why Anthony Browne's prediction in the *Observer* newspaper that 'UK whites will be minority by 2100' is only part of the truth.[8] Indeed, to make the matter a 'colour issue' is beside the point and risks giving fuel to racists.

## A grim kind of optimism

I have been at least a little cautious in my choice of terminology. The very last thing I wish to do is to fuel racism. But neither, if we wish to anticipate what *will* happen rather than pontificate about what *should* happen, can we afford the false consolation of denying cultural differences. And the reality is that the largest, most robustly non-assimilating and culturally traditional group within European societies is Muslim. Ironically, of course, it is with precisely this culture that the West finds itself locked most persistently and most dangerously in conflict at the moment. The ramifications of this conflict are so great that we can hardly pursue them here. (Besides, they have already been touched on earlier in this book.) The 'Muslims in question' are, in any case, hardly monolithic and differ from one country to another: mostly Bengalis and Pakistanis in the UK, largely north Africans in France, Indonesians in the Netherlands, over-whelmingly Turkish people in Germany. We need hardly fear some unified Muslim take-over.

The 'growth sectors' of Western populations, then, might be roughly categorized as indigenous (or imported) under-class and certain kinds (especially Muslim) of immigrants and their descendants. The latter, it must be remembered, will inevitably be augmented from outside – probably far more rapidly, indeed, than they generate their own growth. It is these sectors that are slowing the downward drag on the aggregate population caused by the drastic decline of the majority, indigenous middle class, which will swiftly cease to be a majority at all.

What happens then? Presumably at some stage the two presently smaller sectors of the population become the main sectors. But the cultural differences between them will be vast. The indigenous underclass will have been badly socialized as a result of fragmented families and unstable homes. They will not, on average, be candidates to become the new managerial class. The descendants of the immigrants, by contrast, will probably have shared the experience of poverty, but little else besides. Their solid family backgrounds will have given a stability to their lives and a greater disposition to benefit from the education system.

Race riots might safely be predicted for the middle of the century, but the outcome could never be in doubt. The medieval peasant revolts were all foredoomed (no matter how bloody they became) for the very simple reason that their participants were peasants; they possessed no practical alternative programmes and no one capable of implementing them if they had. They were outbursts of impotent fury, nothing more. The uneducated and ineducable can run nothing. That will be as true of the future as it was of the past. The running of everything that matters will pass into the hands of those capable of managing it.

The conclusion we have come to is pessimistic only from the standpoint of racists and fascists. It might well be thought an optimistic scenario – even if rather grimly optimistic. By the late twenty-first century, Western countries will once again be run, and largely populated, by people who subscribe to traditional morality and long-run-of-history, solid cultures. The anti-culture with its anti-values will be nothing but a bad memory; it will be 'one with Nineveh and Tyre'.[9] The fact that the particular form of traditional morality and solid culture is likely to be Muslim is, perhaps, unfortunate – even if (and this is the grim aspect) it is no more than Western barbarians deserve.

In the USA, the situation is somewhat different to the scenario described above. For the US birth rate is 2.1 children per woman – precisely the replacement rate. As Mark Steyn pithily observes, 'America's religiosity, now unique in the Western world, is at least part of the reason it reproduces at replacement rate, also uniquely in the Western world.'[10] But that, of course, is not the whole story. There, it is the differentials between groups within the population that is the key issue – and that is quite explosive enough. Secular, liberal-left, middle-class Vermont has a European-style birth rate of just 1.57; religious, Mormon-dominated Utah runs at a more than healthy 2.71. But it is the rapidly expanding Hispanic population that will be the decisive factor in shaping the future. They may constitute a flood of immigrants, but they are certainly assimilating, at least in the terms we are considering here. (I leave aside the growing issue of language, along with complaints by Pat Buchanan and others of his type about 'alien culture'.) For it was with good reason that Samuel P. Huntington described Latin America as a 'sub-set' of Western civilization. And after arrival in the USA, people from Latin America assimilate to at least some of the mores of the lower end of the social spectrum in their new country. The illegitimacy rate among immigrant Latino new mothers is 37 per cent; this rises to 48 per cent among American-born Latino new mothers. (Illegitimacy rates for the US population as a whole run at 33 per cent.)[11] Other cultural patterns among Hispanics bear greater similarities to North American and European behaviour than to that of, say, Asian cultures. High illegitimacy rates, obviously, are connected with fragmented families and their economic, social and educational consequences. This pattern of immigration might, perhaps, be expected to create a new, extended underclass. The high birth rate and the apparently limitless supply of such future immigrants will probably mean, however, an extended potential lifespan for the Western anti-values within the USA. But the likelihood of race conflict remains, especially as the shifting population balance reaches various critical points, both nationally and locally.

As mentioned above, this last part of the analysis has been at least somewhat speculative, resting as it does on what we know of human behaviour rather than on simple mathematics. And, of course, no allowance has been made for externals such as war or ecological crisis. Indeed, Dr Peter Heslam has privately called into question, not my diagnosis, but my evaluation of it – for Westerners consume proportionately far more of the world's resources than the other inhabitants of the planet do. The demographic collapse of the West, he implies, may not be such a bad thing on ecological grounds.[12] This is a very weighty consideration, for environmental disaster is staring us in the face. I am grateful for his criticism. It may well be that another book waits to be written, elucidating how far, and in what sense, late-modern or post-modern Westernity has failed another acid test of sustainability. It does not, however, strictly belong in *this* book. A few localized environments (degraded at the hands of Western multinational companies) apart, environmental damage is not part of the explanation for 'why the rest hates the West'. The resentments of ordinary non-Westerners are cultural and moral, not environmentalist. Indeed, outside Western countries and the westernized élites of Africa and Asia, environmental awareness is distressingly rudimentary. It is among the poor farmers of Brazil and Indonesia that slash-and-burn continues with, if anything, renewed vigour; it is in the formerly communist states (including China) that pollution has wrought the greatest havoc; it is in southern Asia that smoke clouds regularly obscure the sun for weeks on end.

Of course, it is Western-style industrialization that began this process, and it would be nonsense to suggest otherwise. It is also the West's insatiable appetite for fuel that sustains the threat to our atmosphere. Nevertheless, if salvation from ecological catastrophe is to be found at all, it is from the West itself that it will come. Only there is technology allied with the generalized political awareness that this issue really matters. Neither the technical skills nor the political willingness and ability to implement strong environmental controls are present elsewhere.

In any case, the observation that Western demographic suicide would benefit the environment remains an argument, not for its actual implementation, as for the drastic reduction of toxic emissions, probably best achieved via 'polluter-pays' taxation schemes (or what economists call 'internalizing the externals') and other, probably equally painful, measures. Neither would the demographic scenarios outlined above alter the environmental picture, unless the new inhabitants of formerly Western countries consent to a drastic reduction from present Western living standards. And if they can harness technology to cut environmental impact without slashing living standards, then so can we.

But, however much one may choose to differ from my guesswork or evaluations, what is no guesswork at all is the stark fact that we face demographic meltdown, and that we do so as a direct result of the distinctive features of Western life and the Western world-view.

The central point I wish to make is that, if such a future is to be averted, then it neither can be nor should be on the basis of conflict, racist backlash and iron defences against immigration. For, not only are these things morally wrong, but they cannot possibly succeed in averting the direction that events are taking: that direction is determined entirely by the consequences of the Western anti-culture itself. It is Western amorality that has brought about both the demographic decline and the conflict with traditional cultures. Neither of those things will be reversed by mere nastiness.

Morality and the nature of reality, then, both point in the same direction. C. S. Lewis pointed this out back in 1943 in his classic work *The Abolition of Man*.[13] Morality is built into the fabric of the universe itself; it cannot be expunged, be our technical wizardry never so clever. It can be ignored and sidestepped, he insisted, only at the price of ceasing to be fully human. Perhaps even Lewis did not foresee the full price: that the society that decisively set aside traditional morality ('the Tao', as he called it) would simply cease to 'be' at all.

If Westerners feel uneasy about the demographic future we have just been mapping out – and I should stress again that the purely speculative, predictive aspect rests on the decidedly unspeculative basis of mathematics – then there is only one alternative recourse. If Western population levels are to recover, then the behaviour patterns that underpin them have to be recovered too. Nothing less than a massive cultural reversal is necessary. We shall need to rejoin the rest of the human race.

# Conclusion: the renewed relevance of a religious – and moral – vision

The point we have come to is not so much the end of a discussion as the beginning of a new one. To condemn is easy; to construct, difficult. But, in a way, that is part of my point. Since Descartes, doubt has attained increasingly the position of cardinal – and in recent years, almost the only – intellectual virtue in Western life. And I have been expressing doubt about that. I have been deconstructing deconstruction, repudiating our repudiation of the human past, pulling the gun on the culture of debunking and challenging it to produce its credentials – in the confidence that it cannot.

My fun is over. The question arises as to where we go from here. If Western societies are to sustain themselves at all they will, at a minimum, need to reverse their birth rates – and quickly. But to do that, they will need to change the patterns of behaviour that have produced the present situation. This is not a matter for governments – or at any rate, not primarily for governments. The conviction that it is is itself part of the disease from which we need to be cured. We cannot forever pretend that there are technocratic fixes to deliver us from the need to make tough moral decisions. We, in our own persons, are finally responsible for our own actions – and inactions. Like pouting adolescents, we have demanded 'to be treated like grown-ups' – but when, in response, we were shown the washing up and proffered a brush and tea towel, replied furiously that that was not what we meant at all. We meant only that we should have our own way, not that we should accept any responsibility.

We shall need to cease trying to be adolescents into our 20s and 30s (and even beyond), and consent instead to become grown-ups. And to do that, we shall need to be reconverted to the truths about morality, family and social relations that we have lately come to reject as oppressive. We shall, therefore, need to become much less quick to reject each and every claim of duty as being somehow an infringement of our 'rights'. Indeed, we shall need, in the long run, to abandon aggressive self-assertion and the 'rights' ideology on which it is founded altogether.

By abandoning the anti-culture and its anti-values, we remove the real sting that poisons relationships between 'the West and the rest'. By rejoining the human race, we make dialogue, rather than endless, terror-filled stand-offs, possible once again.

This doesn't sound altogether likely, does it? Certainly, from the vantage point of 2003, it sounds rather far-fetched. But we have no other way forward, and so we must take it. But we shall need to be confrontational. Christians, in particular, have been so quick to try to make their peace with the anti-culture that their churches and their own lives have been terribly eroded by it. That must stop. For it will certainly make no peace with them. Supporters of traditional moral opinion are being systematically crowded out of the public square. They are even being crowded out of the churches themselves. Religious leaders make concessions to those who dissent from historic orthodoxy or orthopraxy and find – hey presto! – that, for fear of offending them, they must thenceforward choose their words carefully (and, indeed, silence the vociferously orthodox among their flocks).

The anti-culture begins by pleading tolerance for its anti-values and ends by devouring all who will not say its shibboleths. That is what so angers the Third World today. 'Tolerance' has been radically redefined. Originally it meant that two people (or groups, or institutions) that were divided by hard, non-negotiable difference refrained from oppressing one another on account of it. Now, it has come to mean a dogmatic agnosticism about all truth claims and moral questions, dissent from which is to be hounded at every turn until all submit to its insistent nescience. From being a value, it has become an anti-value. (This, presumably, was why Yale College's administration refused, in 1997, to grant Orthodox Jewish students exemption from its requirement that all live in mixed dormitories – though it had already approved a Bisexual, Gay, Lesbian and Trans-gender Cooperative and special arrangements for ethnic minorities. As the Dean said in defence of compulsory mixed-sex units, they 'embody our values and beliefs'. Precisely so. Morality must be allowed no escape.[1])

Christians, of course, have for some years been making polemical hay with this fact. The new 'tolerance' will not tolerate traditional morality: 'everything is permitted in the permissive society – except, of course, Christianity (or Judaism, or Islam, or . . .)'.

If they are honest, however, Christians must admit that they have not succeeded in pointing out some inconsistency on the part of those who oppose them, as if the latter did not live by their own standards of openness. Rather, the phe-nomenon indicates that the new anti-values are inherently self-contradictory. For no society can live without some overarching framework, or metanarrative – even if it is the metanarrative of anti-metanarrativism, or the absolutizing of relativism.

The only question, therefore, is which we shall choose for our public life: a general framework that upholds tradi-tional morality or one which denies it and, in the process, undermines the basis for perpetuating society into the future. Both options admit of variations within themselves;

the latter does not have a monopoly on pluralism. Neither does the former choice entail a return to the Spanish Inquisition; it might equally well (or rather, much better) be a revisiting of the heady cocktail of Vienna in 1900.

Indeed, if we wish to confront the anti-culture, we shall necessarily find ourselves making an interesting network of friendships. For starters, Western Christians of all kinds – evangelical, high-church, Roman Catholic and Orthodox – can usefully unite behind a commitment to reconnecting with the rest of humanity. And they can do so without in the least pretending that they agree with one another about all – or, indeed, about any – of the things that have historically divided them. That was the folly of the ecumenical movement; rather like the Jehovah's Witnesses prophesying the Second Coming for 1975, the British Council of Churches predicted in 1964 that institutional unity between the main denominations would be attained by 1980. If the falsity of the first prediction was rather a shame (rule by Jesus being infinitely preferable to the events that have transpired since the Nixon years), that of the second was an immense relief; technocratic unity on the basis of theological heat-death, with all beliefs relativized to a sort of credal room temperature under the tutelage of an all-wise committee, would have been equivalent to the dispensationalists' Great Tribulation.

Real Christians, meanwhile, have been co-operating, where it suits them, for years, and have been doing so without selling short their beliefs at all. I merely point out that, in our present exigency, it suits us all to co-operate now.

Indeed, we shall need to co-operate with Jews, Hindus and, for that matter, Muslims – not to mention all those people who may have no clear religious faith at all but who can see the need for a cultural reversal. As Professor John Gray, himself an atheist, chivalrously observes, 'One cannot engage in dialogue with religious thinkers in Britain today without quickly discovering that they are, on the whole, more intelligent, better educated and strikingly more free-thinking than unbelievers (as evangelical atheists still incongruously describe themselves).'[2] Well, yes. Not all of the advantages, it would seem, are on the other side.

People who virulently disagree with one another and would not dream of praying together to some vague ecu-deity (or even of praying at all) can nevertheless join, for example, in reintroducing the language of duty to public discourse, in challenging the public authorities to uphold morality, and to stop penalizing marriage through the tax and benefits system. We could be seen visibly to support one another when leaders take a public stance on moral issues.

We could make some personal sacrifices as well. If we believe that refusing to buy products from a company or country of which we disapprove can bring about change, why will we not do the same in refusing to patronize the debased, vile and anti-moral offerings of so much of the media? (I speak as a teacher of theological students whose outlooks are shaped far more by the amoral soap operas whose anti-values they unconsciously imbibe than by the Bibles they aspire to live by.)

Such co-operation will, of course, be a huge joke at the expense of our allegedly multicultural masters. For it will be an exercise in real multiculturalism – not a fake. It will not be the emasculation of cultures in the supposed interests of non-discrimination, but rather of their perpetuation and strengthening. People of real, solid cultures that are sep-arated by hard, utterly non-negotiable difference can nevertheless co-operate, without feeling the need to destroy one another's institutions because, for example, a Christian is not welcome to be a teacher in a Muslim school or a Hindu may not work in a kosher butcher's shop. Adherents of real cultures know that they must be given the freedom to build up and exercise the institutions which, just as with birth rates, are necessary to perpetuate the life of those cultures', and that the existence of Muslim, Jewish and Christian schools are not a prelude to a re-run of the Holocaust.

Mostly, however, we are reduced to personal moral suasion over those around us. The moral climate of Victorian Britain produced, but was not simply created by, moral campaigns and political reforms. Instead, an increasingly religious and moral climate was built up slowly, one issue and one person at a time. Doubtless the process was more synergistic than I am implying here. But my point is that we cannot use public action divorced from personal transformation – there is no ducking the hard graft with technocratic solutions, for the conviction that we can is itself one of the errors from which we need to be delivered.

In seeking to recreate a moral society, we do not need to be bound to the imposition of one religious faith – or of any – as the aggressive secularists would caricature it. In myriad ways, we can – and must – work for the renewal of a moral vision in the West that is rooted, not in a culture of rights but of duties, not of aggressive egalitarianism and brazen sexuality, but of respect and decorum. Religious believers will know the Real Origin of that ethic, and will be motivated by it. But non-believers need not. And, though we may try to persuade them, that is finally up to them. That, after all, is the true meaning of tolerance.

# *Notes*

## Introduction

1 A. Bloom, *The Closing of the American Mind* (New York, Simon & Schuster, 1988), pp. 25–6.
2 P. Crone, *Pre-Industrial Societies* (Oxford, Oneworld Publications, 2003), p. 1.
3 Crone, *Pre-Industrial Societies*, p. 1.
4 All statistics from S. P. Huntington, *The Clash of Civilizations and the Remaking of World Order* (New York, Simon & Schuster, 1997), pp. 85–7.
5 R. Scruton, *The West and the Rest* (Wilmington, Delaware and London, Continuum, 2002).
6 R. Hughes, *Culture of Complaint* (London, Harvill Press, 1994), p. 73.
7 D. Landes, *The Wealth and Poverty of Nations* (London, Little, Brown & Co., 1998).
8 *The Times*, 3 August 1998.

## Barbarian juggernauts

1 *The Times Magazine*, 16 October 1999, p. 10.
2 S. P. Huntington, *The Clash of Civilizations and the Remaking of World Order* (New York, Simon & Schuster, 1997), pp. 68–78.
3 Huntington, *Clash of Civilizations*, p. 51.
4 Huntington, *Clash of Civilizations*, p. 184.
5 O. Guinness, *The Gravedigger File* (London, Hodder, 1987), pp.61–2.

6 D. Lyon, *The Steeple's Shadow* (London, SPCK, 1985), p. 43.

7 T. Paine, *The Rights of Man*, H. Collins, ed. (Harmondsworth, Penguin, 1977), pp. 108–10.

8 J. Gray, 'The myth of secularism', *New Statesman*, 16–30 December 2002.

9 P. Morgan, *Farewell to the Family?*, 2nd edn (London, IEA, 1999), ch. 1.

## On the importance of being earnest

1 Romans 7.18 (AV).

2 Matthew 5.27–28 (NIV)

3 M. Luther, *Against the Heavenly Prophets* (1525).

4 Matthew 6.4,6 (NIV)

5 E. Burke, 'A Letter to a Member of the National Assembly (19 January 1791)' in *The Works of Edmund Burke* (London, 1909–12), II.555.

6 G. Himmelfarb, *The De-moralization of Society* (London, IEA, 1995), pp. 229, 231.

7 Psalm 51.6 (NIV); *Hamlet*, I.iii.

8 M. Luther, WA.I.148.

9 J.-J. Rousseau, *The Social Contract*, tr. M. Cranston (Baltimore, Pelican–Penguin, 1968), p. 49.

## How to be sinless: human rights and the death of obligations

1 P. France, *Diderot* (Oxford, OUP, 1983), p.62 [quotation on p. 63 also shows its weakness].

2 H. Sidgwick, 'Bentham and Benthamism', *Fortnightly Review* 21 (January–June 1877), p. 639.

3 Cited by J. Laughland, 'The new imperialists', *The Spectator*, 25 May 2002, p. 44.

4 S. P. Ramet, *Whose Democracy? Nationalism, Religion and the Doctrine of Collective Rights in Post-1989 Eastern Europe* (Lanham, Maryland, Rowman & Littlefield, 1997).

5 J. S. Mill, *On Liberty* (Harmondsworth, Penguin, 1981), p. 62.

6 J. S. Mill, *On Liberty* (Harmondsworth, Penguin, 1981), p. 63.

7 E.g. Proverbs 31.5,8,9; Ecclesiastes 5.8; Isaiah 10.2; Jeremiah 5.28 (NIV).

8 Romans 9.21 (NIV).

9 1 Corinthians 9.4,5,12,15,18; cf. 2 Thessalonians 3.9 (NIV).

10 John 16.8 (NIV).

## Killing the past: tradition, progress and un-progress

 1 A. S. P. Woodhouse, ed., *Puritanism and Liberty* (London, J. M. Dent & Sons, 1986), p. 54.

 2 E.g. Woodhouse, *Puritanism and Liberty*, pp. 120, 383.

 3 E. Burke, *Reflections on the Revolution in France*, C. O'Brien, ed. (Harmondsworth, Penguin, 1983), p. 117.

 4 T. Paine, *The Rights of Man*, H. Collins, ed. (Harmondsworth, Penguin, 1977), pp. 63–4.

 5 Paine, *Rights*, pp. 181–2.

 6 Cited in R. Nisbet, *History of the Idea of Progress* (London, Heinemann, 1980), pp. 186–7.

 7 Cited in D. Bebbington, *Patterns in History* (Leicester, IVP, 1979), p. 81.

 8 Cited in Bebbington, *Patterns*, p. 85.

 9 Cited in Bebbington, *Patterns*, p. 80.

10 P. S. Heslam, *Creating a Christian Worldview: Abraham Kuyper's Lectures on Calvinism* (Carlisle, Paternoster, 1998), pp. 2, 100.

11 Cited in Heslam, *Creating a Christian Worldview*, p. 41.

12 J. Edwards, *History of Redemption* (published posthumously in 1774), III.vii.1.3; 2.1; 3.1; viii.1–2.

13 T. B. Macaulay, *History of England* (London, Heron, 1967), i.1–2.

14 J. Gray, 'The myth of secularism', *New Statesman*, 16–30 December 2002.

15 C. S. Lewis, *Timeless at Heart* (London, Fount, 1987), p. 20.

## Impersonal states

 1 G. Mikes, *How to be an Alien* (Harmondsworth, Penguin, 1971), pp. 79, 81.

 2 C. Russell, *The Crisis of Parliaments: English History 1509–1660* (Oxford, OUP, 1977), p. 45.

 3 D. Hirst, *Authority and Conflict: England 1603–1658* (London, Edward Arnold, 1989), pp. 31–2.

 4 A. N. Engelgardt, *Iz derevni* (Moscow, 1987), pp. 430-1, and G. B. Sliozberg, *Dela minuvshikh dnei* (Paris, 1933), ii.248–9, cited in R. Pipes, *The Russian Revolution 1899–1919* (London, HarperCollins, 1990), pp. 114–116.

 5 S. Drakulić, *Café Europa* (London, Little, Brown & Co., 1996), p. 97.

6 'Against the Robbing and Murdering Hordes of Peasants, May 1525', cited in E. G. Rupp and B. Drewery, eds, *Martin Luther* (London, Edward Arnold, 1970), p. 122.

7 From the 50th of Luther's Ninety-Five Theses of October, 1517, cited in Rupp and Drewery, eds, *Martin Luther*, p. 22.

8 J. Goodwin, *Lords of the Horizons* (London, Vintage, 1999), p. 52.

9 C. J. Sommerville, *How the News Makes Us Dumb* (Downers Grove, IL, IVP, 1999), p. 138.

### Imagined communities

1 R. Pipes, *The Russian Revolution 1899–1919* (London, HarperCollins, 1990), pp. 91–2.

2 J. Gow and C. Carmichael, *Slovenia and the Slovenes* (London, Hurst & Co, 2000), p. 11, fn. 23; p. 17.

3 N. Malcolm, *Kosovo: a Short History* (London, Macmillan, 1998), pp. 231, 235.

4 Pipes, *Russian Revolution*, pp.109–110.

5 W. Connor, in J. Hutchinson and A. D. Smith, eds, *Nationalism* (Oxford, OUP, 1994), p. 39.

6 P. S. Heslam, *Globalization: Unravelling the New Capitalism* (Cambridge, Grove Books, 2002), p. 11.

### Divided lives, infantilized culture

1 T. McDaniel, *The Agony of the Russian Idea* (Princeton, New Jersey, Princeton University Press, 1996), p. 47.

2 P. Morgan, *Farewell to the Family?*, 2nd edn (London, IEA, 1999), ch. 1.

3 *Romeo and Juliet*, I.iii.

4 P. Laslett, *The World We Have Lost* (London, Methuen & Co, 1965), pp. 84–92, 285–6.

5 W. Shalit, *A Return to Modesty* (New York, Simon & Schuster, 1999), pp. 204–5.

6 From *Any Questions?*, BBC Radio 4, 10 May 2002.

7 Shalit, *Return*, pp. 58–80, 142.

8 Shalit, *Return*, p. 132.

9 See A. Bloom, *The Closing of the American Mind* (New York, Simon & Schuster, 1987), p. 146.

10 J.-P. Sartre, *Existentialism and Humanism* (London, Eyre Methuen, 1978), p. 34.
11 Shalit, *Return*, pp. 210–11.

## Observations in passing? The demographic trump card

1 Plato, *Symposium*, 191, a, d–e.
2 P. F. Drucker, *Management Challenges for the 21st Century* (New York, HarperBusiness, 1999), p. 44.
3 P. Wallace, *Agequake* (London, Nicholas Brealey Publishing, 2001).
4 P. J. Buchanan, *The Death of the West* (New York, St Martin's Press, 2002), p. 24.
5 G. Dench, *The Frog, the Prince and the Problem of Men* (London, Neanderthal Books, 1994), pp. 21–2, 161–2.
6 T. Dalrymple, *Life at the Bottom* (Chicago, Ivan R. Dee, 2001), pp. 25, 150, 152.
7 Dalrymple, *Life*, p. 42.
8 *Observer*, 2 September 2000.
9 Rudyard Kipling, 'Recessional'.
10 M. Steyn, 'Europe is dying, and the Yanks are going home', *The Spectator*, 15 March 2003.
11 See also National Vital Statistics Report, vol. 49, no. 4 (6 June 2001), pp. 5–9.
12 Private conversation, 3 February 2003.
13 C. S. Lewis, *The Abolition of Man* (Glasgow, Collins, 1978), pp. 14–16.

## Conclusion: the renewed relevance of a religious – and moral – vision

1 W. Shalit, *A Return to Modesty* (New York, Simon & Schuster, 1999), pp. 61.
2 J. Gray, 'The myth of secularism', *New Statesman*, 16–30 December 2002.